T0277191

Praise for crash course

"*CRASH COURSE* will make you realize that failures are your friends. They teach you a lot—and also teach you about yourself. How you deal with them will determine your success."

—DANIJEL VIŠEVIĆ
General Partner and Cofounder of World Fund

"IT'S HARD TO PAY attention to someone's mistakes when you haven't heard of that person, but once I gave *Crash Course* a chance it turned out to be a very easy read. I realized 90 percent of us founders will relate more to this story than to one from Mark Zuckerberg."

—MARC ROVIRA
Founder & Co-CEO of Polaroo

"YOUR BOOK IS very inspiring. I admire your trust in your vision of wanting something different. It's very open minded and evolved, like a capacity of seeing further. It's your gift! Your consciousness."

—JHOHANA BALLESTEROS
Founder of Yo Elijo & Isha System Facilitator

"*CRASH COURSE* builds up as you read. I got so much value in the latter chapters in which I felt you were finally giving us founders the treasure of your personal spiritual journey."

—SEBASTIAN JARAMILLO
CEO and Cofounder at Pinbus.com

"DIVE INTO *Crash Course* by Ricardo Jiménez, where entrepreneurship meets spirituality. This concise guide unveils the profound synergy between business acumen and soulful principles. A game-changer for entrepreneurs, it redefines success as a holistic journey in which the heart leads and financial achievement is trusted to follow."

—GRACE RAMÍREZ
Chef, Author, Entrepreneur & Global TV Personality

"PARADOX, PERPLEXITY, ambiguity—those are some of the words that don't fit the stories around startups, but which are part of it. Ricardo crashes into reality and shows vulnerability and how difficult it is to cope with failure but above all, he shows what you can learn with it!"

—RICARDO PIRES
Angel Investor & CEO of Semapa

"WHAT A POWERFUL story *Crash Course* is. Ricardo Jiménez shares the unvarnished truth. Entrepreneurs rarely share their emotional journeys with failure. Vulnerability is hard. Hiding behind a façade, the actions of others, strict NDAs, make-believe outcomes, or new opportunities is easy. Expect page-turning plot twists that will teach you more than every self-help business book combined on the real challenges and rewards of entrepreneurship."

—MICHAEL RODOV
CEO and Founder of AdNode

"IT'S *SO* REFRESHING to cut the BS and be honest about failure. Everyone speaks about 'speaking about failure,' but barely anyone has the guts to do it, especially not so publicly. A refreshingly honest look at what being an entrepreneur *really* means. Conveying the lessons he learned by embedding them in humor while telling his own story makes *Crash Course* a genius page-turner."

—SOPHIE SPITZER
Head of Education of AustrianStartups

"RICARDO SPEAKS about the unspoken, the silent pioneers—those who are bold enough to build companies yet sometimes are left behind. *Crash Course* felt like a warm embrace."

—ANA-MARIA PRICOP
Cofounder of Outdid.io & Sigma Squared UK Coexecutive

"BUILDING A VENTURE is like climbing a first ascent up a mountain. It is a constant uphill struggle, with avalanches. It demands sacrifice. It takes a team to get to the summit. Often, the team does not summit. But regardless, if the team returns to base camp, they have valuable lessons to share from their journey. The first ascents of Everest or the North Face of the Eiger were possible only thanks to the lessons learned from the many failed attempts prior. The same applies to creating a company. In *Crash Course*, Ricardo Jiménez tells his story and shares the lessons he learned the hard way."

—OMAR BAWA
Cofounder of Goodwall

"YOU'LL NEVER read a book so raw about challenge, sacrifice, failure, and triumph. Ricardo is masterful in turning obstacles into opportunities and helping entrepreneurs avoid the same pitfalls he learned along his career."

—MARCUS LANNIE
Cofounder of Redcoat AI

"*CRASH COURSE* is the perfect guide for anyone who wants to start a company or has had some struggles in their role as a founder. It's remarkable how Ricardo openly shares his story and lets others benefit from his experiences and learnings. Almost everyone will go through something like this in their journey as entrepreneur. My takeaway: Trust in yourself, follow your heart, and you will find your path."

—ANDREAS TSCHAS
Founder of Pioneers.io & Glacier.eco, Keynote Speaker

"WHAT LESSON is better learned than through hardship, and failure. Building resilience and humbleness along the way surely makes the best leaders! The startup world will learn a lot by reading Ricardo's book. I can't wait to share it with all the entrepreneurs and investors to build compassion."

—LAURA COPPEN
Sustainability Investments at H&M Group Ventures

"*CRASH COURSE* seamlessly merges spiritual wisdom and business savvy, providing a lesson-packed road map to prosperity with purpose."

—DAVEN MICHAELS,
New York Times *Bestselling Author & Thirty-Year CEO*

"DIVE INTO the world of entrepreneurship with *Crash Course*. Packed with practical wisdom and raw stories, this business memoir is your shortcut to understanding the emotional angle and non-linear path success often takes. Whether you're a budding entrepreneur or a seasoned pro, Ricardo equips founders with the vision of the inner game you won't find anywhere else."

—AMIT PRADHAN, *Founder and CEO of Rainfall AI & General Partner of JetVentures*

"WE, AS ENTREPRENEURS, are a special kind. We're driven by big dreams, willing to risk it all, and suffering through pains and setbacks. Even at the end of the journey, it might not be the big pot of gold we are hoping for. But there might be valuable lessons for us to jump-start another venture and reach our destiny in ways we didn't intend or even dream of. Ricardo's story is as raw and authentic as it is valuable. It recounts the ups and downs of a founder's journey and gives great lessons and hope for anyone dreaming of becoming an entrepreneur."

—JIA JIANG, *Bestselling Author of* Rejection Proof, *TED Speaker, Top Keynote Speaker on Rejection and Resilience*

"FOUNDERS CAN become like robots, but Ricardo reminds us of what is important, which is to take care of our physical and mental health. Operating from that place will make you an even better entrepreneur. This book is so needed. We are more than our company is what I took from it. Reading *Crash Course* made me feel someone else experienced what I experienced in terms of burnout. It was so authentic, but with you it wasn't a buzzword. Ricardo Jiménez presents a candid insight into personal development, guiding readers to burst the bubble of idealism and evolve into more aware leaders. This shift fosters a life of equilibrium, transcending the cult of busy to rekindle a life of deep purpose. As a friend, I can attest to the authenticity of his words. He brings a presence filled with love to every setting. I could relate to it and other top performers will be able to relate and give themselves the present of being themselves. His profound compassion and dedication extend well beyond that of a driven entrepreneur; he is a mindful leader who generously shares his love and profound wisdom with the world."

—**LEON FORD,** *Cofounder of The Hear Foundation & Author of* An Unspeakable Hope

"RICARDO'S WISDOM and heart first approach as our investor has been a superpower during the best and worst of times for us at Snowball. It helped us earn $8 million with only $2 million raised and turned the bear market as one of the best opportunities for us while others were failing. This wisdom can be captured in his new book."

—**PARUL GUJRAL,** *Founder & CEO of Snowball*

"WE GLEAN more from our mistakes than our victories. *Crash Course* masterfully recaps them all, offering a personal and emotional perspective that resonates deeply. This inspirational journey serves as a powerful ode, reminding us that the very act of navigating through challenges is a triumph in itself—a testament to the resilience of the human spirit. A must-read for those seeking wisdom and motivation on their life's journey."

—IVAN FERNANDEZ,
Founding Partner of Enzo Ventures

"IN THE THROES of World War II, an invaluable lesson emerged from the debris of battle: understanding failure is pivotal to success. The Allies, upon observing the returning fighter planes riddled with bullet holes, initially thought to reinforce the most damaged areas. However, mathematician Abraham Wald shifted this perspective, suggesting that true resilience lay in strengthening the areas untouched by gunfire—the very reason these planes made it back. This insight transformed aerial warfare. *Crash Course* offers a groundbreaking perspective on entrepreneurship, akin to Abraham Wald's WWII insight that understanding and reinforcing unseen vulnerabilities lead to resilience. By candidly sharing his startup's failure, Ricardo illuminates the overlooked pitfalls in the entrepreneurial journey. This book isn't just about building a startup; it's about fortifying it from the inside out, making it an essential guide for anyone looking to navigate the complexities of entrepreneurship successfully."

—SARI STENFORS
PhD, Forbes Futurist & Serial Entrepreneur

crash course

A Founder's Journey to
SAVING YOUR STARTUP AND SANITY

Ricardo Jiménez

Forefront
B O O K S

Published by Forefront Books, Nashville, Tennessee.
Distributed by Simon & Schuster.

Library of Congress Control Number: 2024904355

Print ISBN: 978-1-63763-296-3
E-book ISBN: 978-1-63763-297-0

Cover Design by Bruce Gore, Gore Studio, Inc.
Interior Design by Mary Susan Oleson, BLU Design Concepts

Printed in the United States of America

Dedicated to my parents:
Your unconditional support
always made me feel
I was doing my
entrepreneurial backflips
with a safety net.

contents

The only joy in the world is to begin.

—CESARE PAVESE, Italian author

Introduction

....

I was a startup founder, and I failed.

That's not much of a public admission. Most entrepreneurs don't become millionaires. The reality is that 90 percent of startups don't succeed in the long run, and 10 percent go out of business in the first year.[1] You don't hear much about those, though, do you? We mostly hear about the wildly successful startups that bring unique products and services to the market and change the lives of consumers—and the lives of those who created the company, along with their early investors.

Sadly, that's not my story.

But even though I failed, I want to share my experience. There is no shortage of books about entrepreneurs who kept trying and trying and finally achieved the kind of wealth and market saturation that fuel every startup founder's dreams. We take inspiration from those stories and a belief that we might achieve that kind of success ourselves. There is much to be learned from failure, too, but we just don't hear those stories very often. People usually don't want to experience someone else's misery. Who would? We have enough troubles to deal with in our daily lives without spending energy processing a stranger's sadness because their company fell on its face.

And yet, we might want to reconsider that we can learn valuable lessons from someone else's struggles.

Just because you have the will and fortitude to keep trying doesn't mean you will eventually succeed (or that you should even keep trying). I want to help people understand and grow from the value they can extract from *not* succeeding. There are enough stories about entrepreneurs who lived their American dreams, but what about those of us who put ourselves on the line, worked endless hours, did everything we could to give our companies life, and still faltered and lost our money without ever creating a truly profitable enterprise? That's not a story people usually want to hear, but I am convinced it's important—maybe even *more* important than endlessly studying Cinderella-like success stories. That's what prompted this book: my personal realization that failure can inform a different narrative of success.

Let me start by saying something you already know, which is that there is no formula for winning at entrepreneurship. Tim Ferriss, author of *The 4-Hour Workweek*, created his own personal, unofficial MBA course by taking the estimated tuition cost of $120,000 for an MBA degree and, instead of taking the classes, invested that amount in startups. He argues that you can learn more from the investment experience than you would in the classroom.

"The two-year plan was to methodically spend $120,000 for the learning experience, not for the ROI," he says.[2]

Introduction

I did both. I spent that amount on my MBA from a top business school and then, years later, I created my own personal MBA by investing that amount in one startup—my own. That really is a personal MBA—on steroids.

I spent even more money than that traveling to more than sixty countries (and, sometime later, investing capital in ventures).

I certainly failed at the ROI part...but not at the learning part.

And experiences, you ask? Well, I wonder if I had a few too many.

Nothing turned out as I expected.

I offer here no recipe for business success because there was no such thing in my company—at least not in the traditional sense. I am not, however, writing strictly about failure either. I'll discuss my emotional journey through all the obstacles and plans that never worked out. I will relate stories of struggle and even mistreatment that shrank my business's chances of becoming much more than an idea. I'll also share many great lessons I learned throughout my six-year campaign to build a viable, profitable company (even though it ultimately wasn't). I want to offer those insights to help others who are contemplating starting their own business.

When I first considered writing this book, I told a few other entrepreneurs about my experience and asked what they thought of me recounting the story of my struggle. Their responses were almost universally positive. Many even expressed relief; they could relate to what I was saying, and they (finally) felt understood.

That surprised me. I felt as if no one had ever spoken about their troubles—or made them public. Too many, it seemed, shared my occasional inclination to lock myself in a closet, curl up on the floor, and hide for a while. That's not an exaggeration. There might be no other response after your biggest customer refuses to pay for delivery of a product or when the marketing agency that promised you the moon ends up delivering almost nothing, blaming their failure on the weather. (That actually happened to me.) Maybe you were deterred by technical vendors who broke up the integration of your website with your fulfillment house, refused to do repairs, and then just disappeared. That happened to me too.

Is that closet starting to sound like a safe space yet?

My greatest hope is that this narrative can provide entrepreneurs with comfort, companionship, and an understanding that whatever you may end up going through is simply life and business, and there is nothing wrong with you. Trust in yourself, follow your heart (which is disguised as a venture) where it leads, and don't fear the outcome, because *you are much bigger than your company*. If I can convince you of that, I'll consider this book a huge success. Never forget that *you* (and your family) come first, and the business comes second. And that's not just a mental health principle; it's a business principle. By remaining healthy and optimistic, you are more likely to reach your goals.

Introduction

Before starting my business, I read *The Art of the Start* by Guy Kawasaki. A friend recommended I spend time with the book, and I'd offer the same advice to any entrepreneur beginning their own journey. Kawasaki's message is motivational and will help you kick things off. While his great success lessons will get you rolling "making meaning" and changing lives,[3]

Trust in yourself, follow your heart (which is disguised as a venture) where it leads, and don't fear the outcome, because you are much bigger than your company.

I hope what you find here will keep your tires and your spirit from deflating when things don't go well along the journey.

I also recommend having at least a one-sentence plan for worst-case scenarios. My approach was to outline three potential outcomes that included the optimistic, the realistic, and the pessimistic. You can also transcend the extremes on either end of my scale. That was in the business plan. My situation became far worse than I could have imagined, and I'm not just talking about the cold numbers on a spreadsheet. The emotional swings and dark moods were also problematic. I never expected to feel so lost and overwhelmed. It was very important in those moments to have already articulated the worst-case scenario, which, for me, was having to sell my house to pay my company's debts—knowing I could live/be okay with that. Some nights, holding on to that—my personal worst potential outcome—was the only thing that enabled me to sleep at night. Oddly, I think it also increased the likelihood of my success.

Reading about someone else's failures and struggles may seem strange. It might feel like a cautionary tale or a warning against chasing your dream. That's not my intent at all. I do not want to deter anyone from going after their dreams. My goal is to share my experience in the hope that you will be able to see the main square of the town from a different balcony. And if reading this book prompts you to skip the emotional pain of starting a company that might fail—and, according to the odds, it probably will—then maybe it will have accomplished an important task of helping by showing a potential outcome that others may be able to avoid beforehand. Fail fast, as they say in the startup world.

Of course, I will admit up front that no such book would have stopped me from launching my company. Like most new entrepreneurs, I was stubborn and naïve. Stats did not apply to me, and misfortune and difficulty were not going to apply to *my* startup. Those were the problems of less-capable people with less-shiny ideas. I was pushed ever forward by the brilliance of my thinking and my capacity to "make it happen." I jumped in knowing that, even if the worst outcome happened, I was committed to pressing on to see things through for myself…all the way to the end.

And that's what I did.

SECTION 1

Beginning with an Ending

chapter 1

I Demand Euphoria

....

THE DECISION HAD been made. I was going to start my own company. My background included enough education, business expertise, and life experience to give me the confidence to succeed, and I started by seeking the advice of professionals in the booming tech city of Austin, Texas.

Unfortunately, instead of feeling like an entrepreneur in charge of my own personal destiny, I began to see myself as everyone's bitch.

One of my first meetings was with a man named Carlos. An associate had suggested he was the right guy to help me launch my sales efforts and grow my revenue. His resume was impressive enough over the course of his twenty years in business that I was excited about the possibility of a collaboration. We met at a restaurant not far from his house, a location he frequented because of its tequila selection. I, of course, was picking up the tab.

"So, tell me about your product," Carlos said.

"Well, it's something that both parents and children will

be interested in," I said. "I think that's what gives it so much market potential."

"I'm not sure I understand."

I offered a bit more detail as Carlos quickly moved on to sipping his second tequila, which I noticed had come from the top shelf. I hoped he wasn't hungry too. I gave him enough information to pique his interest, and he gave me the names of some people he knew from his sales career.

"You think you could introduce me?" I asked.

"I could. But I just can't give away my contacts. I'd need some kind of a retainer to cover my time and the value of my relationships."

"Oh, I see." I leaned against the back of my chair, and he finished off his second Patrón shot.

"I'm sure you understand," he said. "My wife likes nice things, and we've got a lifestyle to maintain."

My shoestring budget could not begin to meet the needs of his spouse, or, for that matter, his thirst for pricey tequila. Instead, I suggested a strong sales incentive, but Carlos was having no part of that either. By the time I walked out the door, I had wasted four hours of my day and more money than I could spare.

I already knew that being an entrepreneur would not be easy and that 90 percent of such ventures fail.[4] I'm sure that statistic is bumped up by first-time entrepreneurs with no real budget or experience—in other words, people like me. We don't, however, hear much about the stories of failed ventures, or, if we do, it tends to be after the entrepreneur has been successful in a subsequent attempt. Then, from this new position of accomplishment, they talk about their past and all the times they failed before they finally struck gold.

My story does not come through the perspective of success.

I will be telling you about failure and all those things the entrepreneur does and suffers through to achieve "success," even if—as in my case—they never get where they want to be as a businessperson. People don't often talk about this path because, unless the struggle culminates in success, the story seems incomplete, not worth sharing, maybe even uninspiring. And don't we expect entrepreneurs at least to be inspiring?

We miss a big part of reality when we view entrepreneurship only through the lens of winning. Thinking of entrepreneurship—or life— as winning or losing is seeing life in black and white. Almost as fantasy, the way women are held to the unrealistic physical standards of Victoria's Secret models and filtered Instagram images of perfection. There is already enough psychological pressure that comes with the noble and challenging mission of building a company where there once was none.

> *We miss a big part of reality when we view entrepreneurship only through the lens of winning.*

Carlos was a symptom of my entrepreneurial disease. Although he was not responsible, I realized that in a matter of just a few weeks, I had begun to question my plans and strategies. I tried to trust myself and the decisions I was making, but when they ended in failure, I had only created more internal doubt. Constantly questioning myself was not constructive and seemed to accelerate things falling apart. I admit I was inspired by the romantic picture of becoming the entrepreneur who creates an innovative product to solve a real problem, improves the lives of half the world's population, and eventually wins intellectual acclaim and wealth as the result of hard work.

But there's considerably more to my business story than failure. To understand my business "crash," you first need to know a bit about my background, which will provide context for what happens throughout this narrative.

For as long as I can remember, something deep inside me has wanted more than what meets the eye. I never knew what that was, but there had always seemed to be something missing in my life, which manifested itself in a subdued feeling of constant dissatisfaction. I suppose I was trying to grasp more than what I could see around me. Whatever that was, I sensed its absence, and I think that had much to do with keeping me from feeling fulfilled. I can't even think of any people I admired or things that impressed me as a child, but maybe that's because I always took everything for granted and had developed almost no capacity for appreciation.

I Demand Euphoria

Before I get too far into my story, I need to make something crystal clear: this book is not about inspiration. My intention is to expose the twists and turns of the entrepreneurial path and the ups and downs I went through. I also want to point out that I am not giving you only a tale of a failed startup. This is not just about the machine being built; it's mostly about the person building it—the entrepreneur—and their emotional journey, because there is a good chance the journey will also be your story if you are choosing the startup life.

This book won't teach you how to fix your business issues. Rather, it will speak to the pains suffered by young, low-budget, first-time entrepreneurs. And you will come to see that feeling like a failure and being overwhelmed are common experiences for anyone starting a new company. I won't spend a lot of time explaining how to build an enterprise, because what I want more than anything is to help you avoid being internally demolished in the name of a goal. This book is not about building the perfect Formula 1 car or winning a grand prix; it's about taking care of the pilot—*you*.

This book is not about building the perfect Formula 1 car or winning a grand prix; it's about taking care of the pilot—you.

I finally came to understand that there is nothing more dangerous to the entrepreneur than a narrow view of reality that tells us that our worth and future depend on the success of our company. We allow this to add a layer of psychological pressure to our endeavors, which creates unrealistic expectations, and we do not need that pain.

I did go into business with one distinct advantage, which was that I knew from the time I was very young that I wasn't going to be sitting in the same office chair for twenty years. I realized this even before I began working at my first paid job for the Spanish airline company Iberia in Madrid.

There were a hundred interns like me who were informed near the end of our year at the airline that continuation with the company wasn't guaranteed, and we were encouraged to look for another job. Fortunately, I had heard about a foreign commerce program offered by the Ministry of Economy in Spain. This seemed like a perfect fit for me because the internship involved spending the first year as a trade advisor in a commercial office in an embassy of Spain somewhere in another country, and a second year working for a Spanish company that had international activity.

I was only twenty-three, and this seemed like the perfect opportunity to begin exploring the world—which was one of my great ambitions. There were only one hundred fifty open positions, and thousands of students from across Spain applied. All of them, like me, were hungry for opportunity and adventure.

I Demand Euphoria

The selection process took months and involved test scores, country preferences, and an assessment of your character, goals, and background. Those who were selected to participate had no real control over where they were assigned. That's how I landed in Indonesia, a country I could barely locate on a map. I was concerned about what my life might look like there, but not enough to let it stop me from exploring the options offered by this experience.

My top two choices had been Rio de Janeiro and São Paolo. I entertained images of broad, sweeping beaches filled with beautiful, sun-kissed women. Instead, I got on the phone with the Spanish intern I was to replace in Indonesia, who told me I was very lucky to get this assignment because the supervisor liked to give his interns plenty of days off so they could travel around Southeast Asia. He also suggested there was great opportunity to meet women and that a certain part of my physiology was likely to become overused.

"Your cock is going to turn into an eggplant," he said a bit bluntly.

Regardless of potential anatomical alterations, Indonesia still seemed not particularly attractive to me and, from my total ignorance, I thought it might be restrictive or even dangerous.

While I pondered the risks of moving to the unknown country of Indonesia, I also considered the possible professional trajectory before me if I were to keep my job with Iberia. The employee my boss reported to was about twenty years older than me, and I had less interest in his job than I did in my intern position. I could not imagine being somewhere for two decades, just to change chairs or offices. I craved uncharted places and engagements that were the opposite of the corporate environment. Ideas such as warmth, a lack of restraint, maybe even a touch of the wild, were what appealed to me. I began to suspect Indonesia might actually be very appropriate for where I wanted to be early in my career.

I felt that I was being true to my heart when I decided to accept the position in Indonesia. I tend to be analytical about my decisions, which can lead to indecision, but I knew what was right for me early in my professional life. I did not know, however, what my passion was—or even if such a thing existed for me. My friends were clear that they wanted to be teachers and engineers and judges. I had no such certainty, and if I ever felt an inkling of it, the conviction was brief and rarely lasted more than a few weeks. There was pressure, though, or it was implied, because I felt like I was part of an educational assembly line and needed to move on to the next machine to be properly molded into whatever I was to become. As a result, I chose my early career without passion. I had to write it down on a college application and could not leave the space blank.

Maybe I had character flaws that led me to become an entrepreneur. As a teenager, I don't recall myself being curious. I remember spending a few days with my friend Juan and our families when we went on a field trip to collect edible wild mushrooms. Juan studied and classified the samples and, when he presented his project to our classroom, the teacher adored his effort and even built a lesson around his findings. My friend was celebrated, and I was just the guy who'd gone along on the trip. I was not interested in those mushrooms. Was there something wrong with me, or was Juan simply a standout? I don't think I ever figured that out.

Maybe I just mistook certain activities for work. I know this attitude or perspective had caused me to lose many chances to engage with people and life in new ways. When I studied at Duke University, I thought my friends were crazy for trying to join multiple student clubs when I felt as though keeping up with the classroom workload was more than enough responsibility. Eventually, I understood that it was possible to find time for extracurricular activities, and my friends may have had more fun than I did even with a bigger commitment load. Looking back, I wonder if I was properly engaged with life. Maybe I was just disconnected and didn't realize it, lost in my little world.

I did have passions, though, which absorbed me from time to time. I exchanged a flurry of correspondence with my favorite music artist from North London during my early twenties, and I wrote multiple saccharine love songs about girls I had met. I suppose that made me similar to every other young man coming of age, not understanding romance but hurting over a relationship that didn't exist, which did nothing for my confidence. I was also a bit behind in making money. I didn't make my first dollar until I was twenty-one and working at a Starbucks in downtown London.

In some areas of life, though, I was already flying. I was only eleven the first time I went to England as an exchange student, traveling without my parents. I got on my first airplane before my father ever took a flight himself. I was fortunate to spend summers with exchange families in English-speaking nations, and the number of countries I visited was well above average for people far older than me. When one of my regular customers at Starbucks in London told me she liked my "cosmopolitan accent," I felt like I might be on my way to becoming a citizen of the world.

These kinds of early experiences inform who we become as adults, and I have needed to look back on my life to understand many of the decisions I made. I'm not sure where my confidence originated when I explored foreign locales without any fear or even apprehension. There were times when I ended up in risky situations that could have been avoided, but I relied on what I considered my wit, charm, and resourcefulness to deal with precarious circumstances.

I did have some minor underlying anxiety and was not in touch with my physical self. I had many unfulfilled dreams, too, which is normal for young people. My self-image, though, was that my mind was stronger than my body, and I perceived myself as intelligent, creative, and even a bit visionary.

But I didn't yet have the success I envisioned for myself, and I felt a disconnect between who I was in my head and who I was in real life. It felt like I was driving somewhere but didn't know where I was going. I was pressing the accelerator with one foot and the brakes with the other all at the same time. Unchanneled energy consumed me from the inside. I wanted —I *needed*—more. I was the living embodiment of an old *Calvin and Hobbes* cartoon I had pinned to my wall. "That's the difference between me and the rest of the world," it said. "Happiness is not good enough for me. *I demand euphoria!*"

I'd settle, however, for independence, freedom, plenitude, maybe a bit of ecstasy, followed by a touch of rapture. Who wouldn't? My ideals were probably unrealistic. I had a desire to create, to express myself, and to live in possibility. Envisioning a twenty-year tenure of sitting in an office chair waiting for a promotion never was my definition of success.

There are three common traits found in successful people as explained by entrepreneur Alex Hormozi that describe my personality since I was a young kid with more nuance than I ever could have:

> "One, that these people have superiority complex. They believe that they are better than everyone else. They have a bigger vision because they think they deserve it.
>
> "The second thing is they have crippling insecurity. Which is a paradox of paradoxes. They feel they'll never be enough, and they will always be measured against the things that they achieved.
>
> "So you have this crazy dynamic between they think they are better than everyone, they want to go

after this big goal but at the same time they fear they will never actually achieve it and they actually suck.

"And the third piece, which adds the beautiful mix to this is impulse control. They are able to control their actions and focus on a single thing for an extended period of time.

"So, if you put these three things together, you have a big goal that is pulling you this way, you have this big fear that you are running away from, and you have impulse control to keep you focused on the thing that matters."[5]

As important as what we are trying to accomplish is the place from which we are acting. Are we doing something because it's meaningful for us or because we want someone else's approval?

I attended a major university and earned a master's in business administration (MBA), but the idea of knowing what I wanted to be "when I grew up" was debilitating to me. There was too much pressure involved in figuring out something that important before I had acquired the actual clarity to make such a decision. Why can't we just be open and joyful, explore life and career possibilities, and do what makes sense in the moment, day by day, year by year? Why the absurd rush to define our futures and make them an aspect of our personality at such an early age?

What began to emerge for me was a notion that had never once occurred to anyone else in my family. My dad, now retired, was a doctor for forty years. My mother practiced law for fifteen years, became a judge, and has sat on the bench for a quarter of a century. My uncles were teachers or worked as public officials in hospitals. My grandmothers stayed home and raised their children. One of my grandfathers studied chemistry and spent his entire working life in a leather company. The other grandfather traded horses in a village, which, I suppose, is as close as any member of any generation in our family came to being an entrepreneur or a businessman. My two brothers are teachers in public schools, and my cousins became engineers and pharmacists who found corporate employment and never left.

I cannot recall anyone on either my mother's or father's side of the family who had been in business for themselves, and yet I think I was well-prepared to build a company out of nothing. My experiences were supplemented by my ambition to achieve financial and personal freedom. My dream might not yet have been fulfilled, but it was beginning to become clear to me I was suited to be an entrepreneur.

Maybe I could achieve happiness and even begin to approach that whole idea of euphoria with my future successes. That didn't seem like an unreasonable goal . . . at the time, anyway.

What I got, however, would certainly not be described as *euphoric* by any sane person.

Instead, I was about to be taught some of life's hardest lessons about business and people.

chapter 2

Moving Counterclockwise

....

YOU CAN'T BE an entrepreneur without an idea to build a business. I had been entertaining various concepts and products for several years, but there was one I found particularly attractive. I thought it was the simplest and most fascinating idea since twist-off beer caps.

When I look back on that idea these days, though, I have to scratch my head and wonder what I was thinking.

The product: counterclockwise clocks.

I know it sounds absurd, but I was so certain of the global demand and the brilliance of my thinking that I kept the concept completely to myself.

Yes, a counterclockwise clock is counterintuitive and yet extremely simple. Do the very same thing you've always done...but do it *backward*.

The idea seemed appealing to me. Everybody would want one of these clocks, and not just as a novelty to prompt conversation with guests. I saw the entire world learning to tell time backward. I worried, though, that anyone who understood the inner mechanisms of a clock—the gears and springs and their assembly—would be able to easily steal my precious treasure.

I learned a quick lesson about ideas from this clock scenario I had been contemplating. While attending a party with my friend Juan, I shared my idea with him. He was the perfect person to give me informed feedback because he had been doing well in the watch export business in China. I suppose his reaction was more quizzical than enthusiastic, which I expected, but the next day he told me the backward clock was already on the market. I was briefly devastated because I had been certain that if I hadn't heard of that kind of a clock, surely it would have never occurred to anyone else in human history.

I quickly learned the value of spending five minutes on Google doing minimum research before trying to convince myself I had a culturally transformative idea. I also immediately understood that keeping ideas to yourself is not productive because other people must buy into your vision if you are going to eventually get funding. Hiding an idea is stupid for numerous reasons:

- If the idea alone is all you have and you lack a competitive advantage to turn that idea into a business, you have nothing.

- Nobody cares about your idea until they have been

convinced of its value. Plus, people are already busy being absorbed by their own ideas.

- You can look naïve and clueless, stuck in a defensive position instead of going on the offense and giving your idea a chance to get legs and go live in the marketplace.

- It's better to be promotional and proactive, pushing your idea and seeking feedback.

I considered myself fortunate to have a friend like Juan. We had been pals since early in our high school years and had also studied business at the same university in our hometown of Zaragoza, Spain. The year I went to Indonesia on my foreign commerce scholarship, he was dispatched under the same program to South Korea. We traveled together a great deal that year around Southeast Asia, and our friendship only strengthened. Juan was a risk-taker and had been selling various items since he was a teenager. I suppose I was fortunate he was in the watch business and could give me an honest assessment of my backward idea for backward clocks and thus save me money and angst.

Realizing my fortune would not be found in counterclockwise clocks, I went back to Austin, Texas, to continue working and looking for a job that would set me up to become an entrepreneur.

Juan and I continued to talk about the kind of company

we could build together. We agreed it had to begin as a side hustle and needed to be a concept or product we cared about and could scale. I did not want to start a company just for the challenge of it; I wanted a business that fed my creative urges and self-expression and had the potential to become my ticket to freedom.

The problem was, I had no sense of how well-suited I might have been to any particular career. There was little about myself I considered athletic or exemplary in anything physical. In fact, I saw myself as physically weak and shied away from competitive sports because I was afraid of getting injured through engaging in violent physical contact, lifting heavy weights, or performing explosive athletic movements. I didn't have artistic talent, either, nor was I interested in law or medicine like my parents. Engineering was moderately intriguing but seemed unnecessarily challenging. After eliminating a lot of options, I finally landed on a business major in college.

I was as surprised as anyone when I chose to pursue a business degree. I'd always loved good products, but the business side of those products had never appealed to me. I saw myself more as a creative—an inventor, perhaps. Things such as reviewing revenues, profit margins, supply chains, distribution, and branding were not familiar to me. In school, I realized my view of business was childlike and that I lacked any real understanding of what a career in business actually looked like.

My ignorance was a bit more profound than I realized.

Even after studying a four-year undergrad business management curriculum at my hometown university, I had still never even heard the term *entrepreneur*. The concept was not part of the Spanish culture I grew up in. The first time I remember hearing someone say *entrepreneur* was when I was applying for graduate business schools in my late twenties. On one of my first days at Duke University, where I had been accepted into the MBA program, I asked a member of the Entrepreneurship and Venture Capital Club the difference between *entrepreneurship* and *venture capital*. That's when I realized I was beginning the race long after the starter's gun had gone off.

I think, in the wake of the COVID-19 pandemic, businesses around the globe came to realize the most recent generation of workers doesn't want just to be a cog in a big corporate machine. As grateful as they might be for careers and jobs, trudging into an office after their morning commute can lead to feelings of claustrophobia.

I didn't want to feel tiny and replaceable.

My desire was to make an impact, but I equally craved freedom and independence. I realize this can be considered unrealistic by those who can only imagine the world in its current form, but I've always wanted to respond honestly to what I felt in my heart instead of following the cultural pressure to fit a certain profile for employment. Those were the impulses I understood and felt I needed to follow, even though I also accepted that my destination was not completely in my own hands.

Entrepreneurs certainly cannot guarantee outcomes; we can only put ourselves out there and give it our best to realize our dreams of success.

I took an important step in that direction after I acquired my MBA. I landed a great job in corporate America at the headquarters of a major tech company in North Austin. Obviously, there were things I needed to learn, and this would be an ideal environment to prepare me. The campus was full of smart and engaging people, and many of them became my friends. I met people who had been working there for twenty years and some who were quickly moving upward in the organization toward important roles. There were also countless others who had preferred to stay where they were, do their jobs, keep their heads down, and coast along under the radar until retirement.

Entrepreneurs certainly cannot guarantee outcomes; we can only put ourselves out there and give it our best to realize our dreams of success.

Neither of those options was the right fit for me.

I never wanted to "marry" my employer's company and build a life around minimal scheduled vacations, nine-to-five hours, and corporate rules. I did, however, stay open to learning everything I could about the important operations of a big business.

There was much to take in regarding finance and online marketing, the two main parts of my job. My confidence began to grow with experience, professional interactions, and travel. I was good at my job but kept wondering if I was being complacent about my ambition to own my own company. The restlessness was still present but work and a reliable income kept it at bay.

I understood—and felt at a cellular level—that I was not cut out for a corporate career. This tech company was a great place to work, and there were always opportunities unfolding that I used to my advantage, but I started planning an exit. My trigger to quit my job was to put $100,000 in a savings account, which I calculated would give me the resources I needed to pay my living expenses while launching my own company. I was determined to be a full-time entrepreneur, creating a product or service I cared about and could easily scale. Four years at my current job had led me to believe I would be able to achieve my goal and have the money I needed to begin my dream of entrepreneurship.

Before I could jump, though, I got pushed.

chapter 3

An Open Door
(That I Was Kicked Through)

....

THE TECH COMPANY I was working for at the time was a massive, multinational corporation that has sustained market share with aggressive sales efforts and careful analysis of metrics. One of its key measuring sticks was employee performance. Almost everyone working in the Austin office's marketing organization underwent a weekly one-on-one review by their manager. Tips were provided for improved performance, and encouragement was offered toward achieving the team's quarterly strategic initiatives.

My one-on-one weeklies had begun to feel a bit routine. I liked my manager, found his feedback helpful, and acted upon it when it was offered. Our meetings were normally held in one of the company's many "team rooms," which were meeting spaces off the main work area. My manager, Josh's, desk was almost right next to mine, and when the time came for our regular talks, we just walked a few feet away to sit at one of the small tables in a team meeting room. It was odd, then, when our meeting one week was scheduled to take place in an entirely different building.

Josh explained he was going to be coming from a different building, but something didn't feel quite right. I was suspicious. A friend in the finance office had told me a few weeks earlier that I ought to start looking for a new job. I couldn't figure out if he confidentially knew I was personally being released or if the company was cutting loose hundreds of employees as part of a cost-cutting measure in the organization.

I arrived early, found an empty room, and messaged Josh the number and location. The space was perfectly accommodating for the two of us, but after he showed up late, Josh insisted I wait there for him while he found a bigger room. I could not figure out why he did not want me to help him search, but he returned about ten minutes later and said he had found an ideal spot. As we walked down the hall, I had an increasingly strange feeling that I was watching something happen to me that I didn't fully understand, even though I suppose it was obvious. I was totaling up the possibilities before we got to that room, but I confess to still being confused. My mind did not want to acknowledge the reality.

When Josh and I finally walked into the room, a man in a corporate logo shirt was waiting for us with paperwork on the table in front of him. There was nothing humane or warm about this man's presence, and even his language was clinical and almost antiseptic.

"With organizational and strategic changes for the future

competitive strength of the company," he said, "the position you presently hold is no longer in the organization's chart."

I had the sense that a corporate lawyer had created this language to say something without really saying it. I suppose it was crafted to be less painful than a simple "You're fired," but it was equally disturbing.

Regardless, I didn't have to struggle to figure out what it meant for me. The corporate focus on covering its butt made things unnecessarily confusing. I was offered a severance package without ever being directly informed that I was being laid off. There was no clarity and certainly no apology for the shock or inconvenience of suddenly being left with no income. It seemed clear to me that the company was mostly concerned about avoiding any liability. I was just a hired hand, employed at the corporation's pleasure.

I had never in my life been let go from a job. A few girl-friends had shown me the door, sure, but I had never before had trouble processing obvious developments and facts. I found myself watching this situation unfold as if I wasn't the central character in this drama. There was an unsettling strangeness about the fact that I was not explicitly informed I was being fired. They just made it clear that I could go home for the day, as if I were expected to infer the facts of what had just transpired so they wouldn't have to tell me in blunt, painful language.

I was not given enough information to grasp the reality of a broad set of circumstances related to my employment.

What would have been wrong with a candid conversation about what I might have done better? Was it my performance, or were they simply treating many employees as corporate assets that needed to be taken off the books? There was not the slightest bit of human consideration. Mostly, they talked about procedures for turning in my laptop and employee badge and how the severance package worked. I think I was still in a state of disbelief when I walked out the door to my car.

Before I was cut loose, I had been spending many of my free hours working on my startup plans. In fact, I'd been taking several steps over the previous two years to realize a launch. Although my goal had been to accumulate $100,000 in savings before leaving my job, I was only about halfway to my goal when I got the bad news. A jump to entrepreneurship would have been more comfortable with a bigger financial safety net. I didn't want to worry about starting a company at the same time I was having to struggle with personal finances. But there was no avoiding the fact I was now in a situation that I did not yet know how to manage.

I am sure there are stages to unemployment grief, and I am certain I experienced more than a few. As frightened as I was, though, there was no risk I was going to be homeless. I had plenty of money to live on while I sought new work. Using my resources to pay the rent and buy food while also launching a startup business did compound my risks, but I didn't think about those options during the two days I spent in shock at home.

An Open Door (That I Was Kicked Through)

There was no avoiding a certain amount of resentment and feeling like a failure. Around the third day —as I began to let those sensitivities go—I started noticing a strange and subtle sensation. It took me a bit to put my finger on it, but it was a peeking feeling of happiness, of liberation. Of not having to wake up in the morning to go spend the day at a place that didn't make me happy.

I began to think about taking control of my future by finally concentrating on envisioning my new business. And I was suddenly excited about what I was starting to see.

I began to think about taking control of my future by finally concentrating on envisioning my new business.

And I was suddenly excited about what I was starting to see.

chapter 4

"What's Going to Feed You, Son?"

THE WORLD FEELS very strange when you wake up unemployed after spending so much time getting an education and on-the-job experience. I was now all alone with nobody requiring anything from me, no longer needed by anybody.

It took several days to understand my emotions regarding where I was between a corporate career and the beginning of my entrepreneurship. It did not take too much time, though, before I realized I was feeling happier and more alive with each passing day. I did feel a bit off-balance with my newfound freedom. I had never been in a situation where I was able to make my own schedule, decide when and where I might have lunch, plan when to work out, or have the freedom to meet up with friends in the middle of the day.

Just as I was adjusting to my new way of life, an opportunity came along that seemed almost ironic. One of my good friends from work, who had learned about my layoff and current state of unemployment, told me he was going to suggest his manager interview me for a new opening at the same corporation I had just left. The role was as a business liaison with Microsoft, a title I might have found a bit sexy just a few days prior.

Professionally, it made sense for me to pursue the job. I would be able to get right back to work at the same level I'd been at before being released. But I couldn't muster an ounce of desire to start updating my resume and filling out an application. My heart just wasn't in it. If I had been offered the position during what turned out to be my exit interview, or if Josh had suggested during a normal one-on-one that it was a smart career transition, I would have very likely said yes on the spot—but that didn't happen.

I also thought it was important to take some time and deconstruct my experience there. When I looked back on my time at the company, I realized there was much I enjoyed and appreciated in terms of the work environment. My teammates and colleagues were smart and friendly, and I made friends who are still a part of my life. The pay and benefits were also competitive for the Austin market, and the company offered me the flexibility to work remotely from home or while traveling. There was also a lot of opportunity to grow professionally and learn about running a business, not to mention the healthcare and retirement benefits, had I chosen to return.

But there were several things I did not enjoy about the job. Leadership was constantly changing direction, and what was considered critical on Monday might become a secondary concern by Wednesday. It was a fast-paced environment, but it suffered from a lack of conviction, clarity, and focus. Executives always seemed to be offering new strategic initiatives and were sometimes hung up on the company's latest shiny new product and launches, such as printers or cell phones, that were quickly forgotten soon after their release. In sports, you want speed, but if you move the ball faster than your team can keep up, all you are going to do is pass the ball to the other team sooner. That's often how I felt, like a headless chicken.

For instance, the time and effort required to give a presentation to a senior executive seemed wasteful to the point of being extreme. Weeks were spent triple-checking work before delivering it to whoever had made the request for the presentation. Everyone below the requester's rank in the company had to provide feedback and sign off before delivery. Often, by the time the deck was scheduled to be presented to senior management, interest in the idea had softened and new concepts were drawing energy away.

Even more maddening were the constant changes of priorities by the finance team. We frequently were instructed at the beginning of a certain quarter that we should concentrate on raising revenue and told we needed to step on the gas. Abruptly, a few weeks into the quarter, we'd be informed we'd gone too far and were advised to "slow down and focus on profitability." I never understood the contradiction or the need to change course. Even though I realized the logic of what we were being asked, I found it emotionally draining not to have a consistent strategy we could trust instead of changing directions every few weeks.

There were constant reorgs, changing the structure of a giant company to sell by product line, then by area—however that might be defined—and often according to a certain type of customer. New rules constantly flowing from new managers became problematic. The joke in-house was, "If you don't like your manager, don't worry, because in a few months you'll have a new one." The number of emails and meetings was daunting. The universe of stakeholders who had to approve projects, or at least be consulted about them, was absurd. We needed permission for anything that remotely affected someone else's business, or at least their sense of authority. Between the interdependencies, egos, and lack of consistent strategy, it became nearly impossible to feel sustainable progress.

I still get chills thinking about the weeks of work a team of fifty people put into the intricate RASCI (Responsibility Assignment) matrixes, only for them to disappear into some shared cloud drive never to be seen again anywhere in the company. There was even an executive assistant who had a to-do list made up of to-do lists. The undulating levels of unnecessary complexity were wearing on me. I knew I could work just fine within the system. I could easily play the game and do a decent job in the short run by being accountable and professional, but there was no way I was going to feel my role was valuable or bringing out the best in me. It all felt like a game I didn't want to play.

"What's Going to Feed You, Son?"

The absurd exercises seemed to multiply. Goals were segregated by days of the week, channel, product, and subproduct. There were "bridge" goals, "stretch" goals, "official" goals, and "real" goals, and we were hardly helped to understand the distinctions. I resisted the increasing degree of complexity because it only seemed to make my job more difficult. I was longing to escape, but every time I approached that decision, my mother's question from my youth echoed in my memories.

"What's going to feed you, my dear son?"

The question was really about how I was expecting to earn a living, because we all need a roof over our heads, don't we? And something to eat. The sad news we learned as we came of age was that most of us had to settle for an unattractive job and a salary or hourly wage that offered little more than drudgery. And this reality is particularly painful for artists and entrepreneurs.

Listening to all the work and lifestyle gurus didn't provide any answers either. The advice to "follow your passion" was meaningless for me because I didn't *have* a defined passion. I was certainly willing to go in the direction of my dreams, but I didn't really know what my dreams *were* with any degree of conviction, which meant I didn't know in what direction to travel.

I suppose I did have one dream, though unrealistic, of playing as an attacking midfielder for the Real Madrid soccer club, but I knew my physical abilities limited any athletic aspirations. Besides, having no talent for soccer would also pose a problem for me playing at the professional level.

I'm not sure passion has to have a form or a name, though. I think we often find ourselves in personal circumstances that come to offer us definition and even dreams. I knew I craved independence and freedom, and as more and more days of unemployment passed, I was distinctly aware that I did not have the willpower to return to a corporate job and cubicle. How can your job be all that special if the company can quickly find someone else to fill your spot when you leave? People— what they can *do* and what they can *dream*—ought to be considered as something more than assets on a company's ledger.

I think we often find ourselves in personal circumstances that come to offer us definition and even dreams.

While I didn't know precisely what I liked doing, there was a great deal of certainty in my mind and heart about what I didn't like—and that was corporate life. An idea was emerging in my mind that there was something out there that needed to be done, and if I didn't put myself to that task, it would never be accomplished.

I know that's a presumptuous and maybe even egotistical notion, but I think it's how a lot of entrepreneurs feel. We have ideas we think no one else will ever conceive (like backward clocks!), and that conviction is accompanied by a sense that we might achieve something beautiful by attempting to execute our vision and our dreams.

I had finally accepted that my desires were rooted in dissatisfaction rather than passion. My heart had never sent me a strong signal about my future. I admit to not having a directed fire. I was more accustomed to saying *no* to heading in one direction rather than an enthusiastic *hell yes!* to heading in another.

At this time in my life, though, there was *something* that was pulling at me, and I had put a name to it. I wanted to be an entrepreneur, design products, build a business, and, ultimately, create my own financial freedom and "make a dent in the universe."[6] I had the experience necessary in business along with an advanced education, and I was determined to put my time, money, and intellect into fully realizing this ambition. Maybe I wasn't completely ready, but I didn't know how to make that assessment. How do you know when the time is

> *We have ideas we think no one else will ever conceive, and that conviction is accompanied by a sense that we might achieve something beautiful by attempting to execute our vision and our dreams.*

right to take a chance? There is no checklist, but I had come to an inevitable conclusion about my urge to become an entrepreneur.

And it was time to try.

SECTION 2

Starting Up

chapter 5

World Friends

....

THE IDEA FOR my startup business came from an obscure comment I had heard several years earlier while attending the MBA program at Duke University. I don't remember precisely what was said, but I recall having an immediate thought that Americans were quite taken with their own country. I had the sarcastic reaction that they were so patriotic, they'd go to bed with America if they could.

The next image that entered my head was a big, plush toy shaped like the US that anyone could hold and cuddle with when they crawled into bed. I thought there was a profit to be made from such a product, though I had no real interest in promoting or profiting from that kind of patriotism.

About a decade passed before that awkward imagery returned, but it seemed to have evolved while I wasn't thinking about it. Juan and I talked often about starting a business together and wanted to develop a product or idea that was focused on our interests and the things we cared about both in our personal lives and in the wider world. We centered our attention not on creating a clever widget to make money. Instead, the dynamic that had sustained our friendship since childhood was that we both wanted to live our lives without boundaries, follow new pathways, and, who knows, maybe even make a difference in the world, whatever that might be. The company we started grew out of conversations related to travel along with an idea that came to me after that moment at Duke.

My conclusion was that a market existed for plush toys that were shaped like countries, and not just ones that looked like the United States. The products would be called *Plushkies*, a combination of the words *plush* and *countries*. Juan and I agreed on the concept because we had both been to more than fifty countries each at that time, and we knew the value and importance of travel. If we could design a soft toy that could awaken in kids curiosity about the world, we could maybe improve the world a little and, perhaps, make money too.

This idea resonated with us. Broadcast news had always been so misguided, in my view, by elevating fear and failures, war, disease, and poverty. What little international news was available to the public always seemed dedicated to conflict and destruction. Juan and I intended to inspire the opposite kind of reactions from people.

Our Plushkies could highlight international connections that occur at the individual and personal levels and awaken wonder about our beautiful planet and its human occupants. We would facilitate curiosity and learning about the cultures of other countries and teach about their music, food, festivities, geographic attractions, and, of course, their people.

I loved the idea of introducing kids to places in the world through toys. This notion inspired me and filled me with motivation. Everywhere I looked, I saw a market for Plushkies. My conclusion was that our product was original, simple, and, yes, even needed. We believed the timing was right, and Juan and I convinced ourselves we were going to conquer the world.

I quickly found a talented designer to bring our idea to life, and we began developing and discarding concepts until we found a workable formulation. We began with characteristics for each toy that included signifiers such as colors of the nation's flag, a star in the location of the capital, maybe a typical hat or indigenous costume, and various elements that highlighted local cultures.

My goal was for kids to make friends internationally, first by offering a collection of toys and then in real life, and thus create a stronger connection to the wider world. Education makes it a lot harder for one country to throw bombs at another because information and sensitivity to the other culture act as humanizing forces. These were only what might best be described as "toy friends," but in my heart I was convinced Plushkies might contribute to changing how we see other people and cultures in lands different from our own.

Each of the plush toys came with a sticker that children could collect and display in a Plushkies passport. The sticker taught the child to say *my friend* and *cheers* in that nation's language, the latter of which I felt was a great word because it was generally associated with food, drink, and celebrations with friends and family.

Austin, at the time, was a tech-crazy town, and while I was interested in employing tech with my product line, my purpose was far greater. My motivation in life had always been derived from my own curiosity, sense of adventure, experience with travel, and openness to new ideas and cultures, along with the diversity of our planet, its people, and their interests. There was no better way to exercise my personal interests, I was confident, than using creativity and play to educate. Plushkies seemed like a perfect product to fill those niches and attract a broad market of buyers.

Those were my motivations, and I was always eager to learn more. I especially wanted to master the craft of entrepreneurship, which

> *My motivation in life had always been derived from my own curiosity, sense of adventure, experience with travel, and openness to new ideas and cultures, along with the diversity of our planet, its people, and their interests.*

prompted me to review notes from my MBA classes at Duke.

The Tech Ranch in Austin, which incubated new companies, offered a program called Venture Forth. I signed up and happily began attending entrepreneur gatherings there and elsewhere throughout the city. I found coworking space to rent while reading what seemed like every published book on entrepreneurship and productivity, which included *The Art of the Start* by Guy Kawasaki and a collection of Seth Godin's books such as *Purple Cow* and *All Marketers Are Liars*. I also dove into a book Juan had given me, *The 4-Hour Workweek* by Tim Ferriss, as well as Blake Mycoskie's *Start Something That Matters,* which I gifted to Juan because I thought it spoke to our vision and the values that came from our lifelong friendship.

My socializing and professional outreach connected me with other energetic thinkers and dreamers, which charged my creativity with even more enthusiasm. Ideas on product development for Plushkies popped into my head constantly. We had the potential to be a player in four lucrative markets: education, travel, designer toys, and collectibles—categories that were worth billions in consumer spending.

I planned to make our initial launch with nation-shaped Plushkies but thought we'd quickly evolve to offering various types of toys shaped like states, cities, and any locale that had a surface or topography—even a college campus. Another technique for connecting a child to the world might be producing an app that let them connect with other Plushky owners anywhere in the world. That would also allow us to create individual social media profiles for each of our toys. My vision for the tech side of the product was wide, and I saw us producing movies and video games with our diverse country characters. Perhaps even someday a theme park! I saw no reason that we wouldn't one day stand toe-to-toe with Walt Disney's legacy parks.

Sure, maybe my joy of being released to become a "creative" was starting to affect my view of reality. That seemed healthy to me, though. I was scheduling full days of meetings, coffees, and lunches with other entrepreneurs, talking to investors, and doing whatever I wanted or felt was needed to feed my ambitions and create the Plushkies company and brand. There was no measuring the excitement I felt about my new life and the sense of freedom that came from relying on my own creativity. When I walked around outside in the middle of the afternoon to take a break from calls, I wondered how many gorgeous spring days in Austin I had spent trapped in a cubicle in the middle of a huge office with no sunlight to warm my skin or my soul.

There was no measuring the excitement I felt about my new life and the sense of freedom that came from relying on my own creativity.

I certainly did not have the resources to match the magnitude of the vision that was expanding before my eyes and across my imagination, but I didn't see that as an issue. I trusted myself to figure things out, which is how entrepreneurs operate. Besides, zero issues had manifested themselves in those early days. Everything felt right, even perfect. I was doing what I was supposed to be doing, and I had one of my best friends as a partner. We had a product to build. Anticipated orders to ship. Processes to refine. A cultural and economic impact to make.

What could possibly go wrong?

chapter 6

Build It and . . . Will They Come?

ONE OF THE popular trends for young businesspeople starting new companies is a mandate to "keep things lean." It's good advice, of course, to spend only on necessities and make choices that allow you to control growth and expenses. Juan and I were fully conscious of our financial constraints, but we thought speed was more important than keeping things lean. We started out fast, convinced that "if you build it, they will come." We never spoke that silly movie maxim out loud but assumed we would ship and sell, and all the customers we needed would be at our command.

We put our focus on the product. There was hardly a thought given to marketing. We had an idea in the backs of our minds about our customer profile, but we never did any market research. The logic was that if we built a product we were proud of, sales would take care of themselves. I saw nothing to worry about, which, obviously, was a flawed way of thinking. Nothing is more important than what the customers want and need. I just assumed I knew what that was without conducting any analysis.

I admit that I enjoyed building the product…but not doing the market research. My interest was in creating a cool brand, making decisions, and moving forward, not in having to think about *why* I was making the choices I was making.

In business school, I had the first rule of marketing burned into my brain: *Start with your customers.* What do they want? What are they willing to pay for? How are they going to use the product? When we started Plushkies, those guidelines sounded like a nuisance. I thought, *Blah, blah, blah. Not for me.* I found all that stuff boring, time-consuming, and messy, and I had the convenient preconception that whatever data we might be able to gather would be inconclusive. There was nothing the market could tell me that would affect our product design.

Another one of my unvoiced assumptions was that the market had no idea what it wanted. I thought of the old (and probably fake) line widely attributed to Henry Ford: "If I had asked people what they wanted, they would have said faster horses."

I've questioned myself regarding market assumptions for Plushkies many times, but I still can't convince myself the consumer has any understanding of what they purchase or even why.

The iPhone might be the perfect example. The first one came out when I was in business school, and I had no interest in the device. It just didn't seem like it was for me. I was fine with the cell phone I already owned. A few years later, when Juan and I were having initial meetings with our designer, I was already on my second iPhone, with many more to come. I was my own best example that the personal insight of consumers wasn't predictive of what the market might demand. I felt liberated to design what I saw was valuable and a good fit for the market that I perceived existed, which was dangerously convenient thinking.

Young companies function around three things: milestones, assumptions, and tasks. Juan and I kept our attention on the next step, which led to subsequent milestones I was confident would validate our assumptions. I don't recall the two of us ever having serious disagreements about needing to complete certain tasks to help us reach our next milestone. Our biggest assumption, which might have been a dangerous intuition, was, "If you build a better mousetrap, the world will beat a path to your door."

I admit I wanted to speed ahead, to reduce our time to market. I wanted to do what I wanted to do. If only I had been more aware that a significant part of my drive came from my disgust at being laid off by corporate America.

I was in pursuit of success with all the acceleration and speed I could generate for myself and Juan. Too much of my professional life had been spent on an inbox and a calendar full of meetings that did not lead to decisions. Creating a business of my own gave me a chance to oversee movement and action.

There might have been logistical challenges in the launch of our company, since Juan was living in China and I was in Austin. However, our geographic locations turned into an advantage—he could visit manufacturing companies in China while I was able to work in person with our designer in Austin. We had a lot of long-distance conversations about what needed to be accomplished and how we were going to operate. Juan and I were very much aligned at the beginning. Our attitudes were complementary, and we agreed on the vision and, generally, the path forward. We did, however, have a somewhat heated discussion on the matter of markets and research during a phone call.

"Market research and analysis is cumbersome, Juan," I said.

"Yes, but we should maybe consider it a bit, before relying on ourselves," he responded.

"I'm open to discussing it, yeah, but I'm not sure it would be the best way to use our time, because we could work hard on this and results might be inconclusive, no?"

"It's a hard choice to make. We can do some research ourselves, but what do we know about stuffed toys for kids?"

I could tell that while Juan was struggling with this decision, he'd go along with my inclinations. I didn't want to push him in any direction, but we did need to be aligned in agreeing upon the best tactics for the company. We had known each other long enough that we almost understood what the other person was thinking and feeling, which is why we both thought our partnership was bound to succeed.

"I guess we should look at time and costs for a basic market analysis, do you think?" I asked.

"Yeah, but we should also do some of our own research online, you know, see what we can learn about how these kinds of toys are selling and stuff like pricing too."

"Sure, that's probably right. I don't know what we can find out about comparable products, but there's probably data we can gather and save ourselves some money."

"Plus, we've both got good instincts," he added. "I think we understand what will make this toy sell."

"We do," I agreed. "And that's why I'm eager to get it made instead of spending time and money on research."

"I know," Juan said. "Me too."

It's easy to see, in retrospect, that we were taking a big risk with our marketing decision, but we thought other details were more relevant. We didn't want to sell a cheap, meaning-less toy with thin margins. We wanted to produce a high-end product that would last a long time and be educational. Plush toys weren't exactly trending in our techy times, but that was not going to stop us from selling the best product we could design out of the finest available materials. These were going to be the most thoughtful toys in the market, and we were confident that buyers would find their way to Plushkies. I thought our potential was substantially validated by original concept plush toys that were already for sale. GIANTmicrobes and UglyDolls were enjoying success, and I was certain they were inferior to our emerging product line. What other validation did I need?

Yes, there was some arrogance in this attitude. Both Juan and I were driven and saw no need to hit the Pause button on our ambitions. Plushkies would always be evolving and the toys improving, and new products would draw more customers. I didn't care about what I didn't know either. I planned to learn what was needed since I was neither a toymaker nor an education specialist. We could get a first-generation Plushky to the market and then make tweaks and improvements in the next iteration. I didn't have the time or patience for long product-development cycles. Juan and I were determined to think big and make quick decisions. We were committed to the company and comfortable with a healthy dose of risk-taking.

It was perhaps risky to start a company with a friend. Juan and I had been close since our high school years in Zaragoza, though, and we trusted each other to be smart and accountable. We also knew that neither of us would evade responsibilities or take shortcuts. The simplicity of mutual trust reduced legal costs and expedited administration. For instance, we exchanged an email agreeing on the percentage of ownership shares of the company. No lawyer or legal document was required. Responsibilities were also quickly divided in a logical manner that would best facilitate our operations and launch. My role was to manage the design and product, the website, and the brand. Because I was in Texas, I would take care of legal, financial, and administrative issues. From

China, Juan would handle logistics, back-end integrations, and manufacturing for our business while still working his own full-time job.

We believed we made an excellent management team and shared a philosophy to go bigger, brighter, and smarter while making tactical moves to grow our company. We were also confident, I suppose, to the point of endangering ourselves with hubris, but who becomes an entrepreneur without the utmost confidence in their vision and plans?

Who becomes an entrepreneur without the utmost confidence in their vision and plans?

I knew that if we failed it would not be because of a lack of energy or financial commitment, and I had planned to pour every penny of my savings into this project. If anything failed, I'd find a way to double down and try again until it worked out or I figured out what was wrong and made the necessary corrections. While I did not recognize failure as a great possibility, I knew I intended to leave all my soul and money and intellect on the field of endeavor. I also knew in my heart that I would have no regrets in the unlikely event our great dream did not materialize.

One of our earliest steps was to begin the process of turning our product from an idea to an actual, physical product. Juan and I researched five factories in China that could affordably manufacture our Plushkies and leave us a decent margin at retail. We settled on three finalists after Juan visited their operations, but the first round of prototypes left us terribly frustrated. Our sense was that we asked for a balloon, and they delivered a spoon. I realize that's a bit of a tortured analogy, but that's how far off their manufacturers were from our vision. Ugly surprises were also revealed in the quality of materials and manufacturing we received, which led us to hire a local consultant.

Another problem arose when we were informed that we needed a minimum order quantity. All three factories required at least three thousand units of each plush toy, and we couldn't talk any of them down from that. It was clear that figure was either a manufacturing standard…or the three manufacturers we were considering were colluding against us.

We planned to start by producing four different toys. Three thousand units of each design meant we needed to pay out of pocket for *twelve thousand units*. We still felt unstoppable, so we boldly placed that massive order for the first factory run.

Maybe we were being too demanding and jeopardizing the success of our company with our requirements, but we were trying to build the most reputable toy business in the marketplace. There were many challenges to that goal. Our US toy, which we named Katie, was turned down by our manufacturers at the factory because they didn't carry silk with the wavy pattern we had selected. Juan and I insisted that the product meet our specifications, though, and our contractors found a way to produce the correct fabric by using a paint process. We passed safety certifications in the US and Europe for the toys, which we noted in the Plushkies passport, and we even bought our silk from South Korea because it was softer. Our determination was creating a better product for our customers.

My myopia about quickly getting our product to market meant I missed key issues that might arise and slow our progress. With limited resources, we often had to make trade-offs on various decisions, which meant choosing the next most desirable product development step or the investment with the biggest impact. These choices opened us up to risks too. I decided to trademark the brand in Europe, the US, and Asia but deferred spending the money to patent the designs. The reality was that without a patent, any manufacturer could copy our design and just add an element such as a hat, and we would have no protection. We certainly did not want counterfeit versions of our toys in stores around the world that might sell for a quarter of the price. It occurred to a friend, Jia Jiang,[7] that if fake versions of our toys were turning up for sale, then we must be a success. "You should be thanking God if they are copying you because that would mean you are on to something," he offered. Ultimately, I decided to deal with that eventuality whenever it might occur. *That's it,* I thought. *Let's deal with first-world problems at their own accord.*

Problems often came out of nowhere, which is the consistent experience of the entrepreneur—or maybe that's simply the way life unfolds.

We had shipped a container of four thousand of our twelve thousand units to England for storage in a UK warehouse. When the boat arrived, we were informed we were lacking a specific kind of import permit. No one we spoke with in various customs operations seemed to have a clear idea of how to get that documentation or how long it might take to clear our shipment for off-loading. Instead of just leaving our toys on the boat, however, we decided to improvise and had the shippers move the products onto the docks and into the warehouses without the needed document. While I don't usually recommend ignoring regulations and red tape, these are the types of difficult calls you need to make as an entrepreneur when you see yourself standing between a rock and a hard place and you want to move forward.

Our toys were safe in storage and ready for distribution, and we were happy to fill out the appropriate paperwork and pay the necessary fees the moment we were informed what was due.

Our partnership grew stronger through these challenges. Juan and I functioned with mutual trust. We were both driven by the vision of our toys out in the real world, not just sitting in warehouses or sketched on computer screens. Never mind that we kept skipping that whole "product and market fit" issue. We were predisposed to speed to market, and we were not interested in composing and analyzing surveys.

I had a vision of the product, and I wanted to make *that vision* a reality—not what the market might tell me it wanted. That would be their idea, not mine. I didn't know how anyone could come up with a toy that was better and reached children faster than Plushkies. The feedback I coveted was what our buyers would tell us after they had purchased a Plushky for their child. I thought it was very smart to ship first and ask questions second.

> *I had a vision of the product, and I wanted to make that vision a reality— not what the market might tell me it wanted.*

Passion and urgency can often lead to a kind of cluelessness, but Juan and I felt we were handling things properly and beginning to kill the entrepreneurship game. A global company was taking shape without using too much of our available capital. Design was set up in Austin with partial headquarters in Spain; manufacturing was properly positioned for distribution in China and Europe and across all of North America—and we had not yet sold a single Plushky.

We had, fairly quickly, created a company with logistics and operations, and it was ready to scale. Even though we didn't yet have cash or revenue to pay salaries, we had also managed to assemble a team of individuals and vendors to bring our dream to life.

We were doing the "build it" part of "if you build it, they will come."

It turned out the second part of that equation would be much tougher than the first.

chapter 7

The Best Team (No) Money Could Buy

....

Nothing is more important to a startup than people. Mostly because without the capital, processes, technology, and know-how that companies develop as they grow, all you are left with as an early-stage startup is a bunch of people and their dreams. The good news is that people are always your most powerful resource.

Even if you have an ingenious idea that seems destined for greatness, you will never get there without the right people to help you execute your plans. Finding them is a big part of the startup challenge. I felt fortunate that I had the good-will of friends and many others who believed in Plushkies. My hiring budget was zero dollars, but I got the help I needed to succeed by sharing my passion and getting others excited about what we were doing.

Strategically, one of the mistakes I made was not spending time thinking about how I'd build a team while growing the company. Fortunately, support came along even

Even if you have an ingenious idea that seems destined for greatness, you will never get there without the right people to help you execute your plans.

though I wasn't searching for it. People contributed their skills pro bono or accepted payment way below their market value. I took this as an encouraging sign of the potential Plushkies had as a growth company. It seemed like people wanted to be part of this project.

The first person we contracted with was our designer. I found Bruce Lee simply by asking around, and I was fortunate to come across such a talent. As is the case with almost every creative, he had his own ideas about advancing our product. One of his proposals was to incorporate animal shapes into our Plushkies. They were originally designed to be shaped like countries, but Bruce thought that making them in animal shapes would add another intriguing element. His creativity tested my and Juan's vision, and Bruce came to understand more intimately what we wanted to offer and began to give us a true actualization of a Plushky toy.

We were able to find the money to pay Bruce for his initial work and then arranged a long-term engagement. I had no idea how much of his talent we would employ over the development of the company, but it was more than we could afford financially. He was essential to the look of our stickers, passports, flyers, flash cards, posters, and each new Plushky. He never charged us for many hours of work, and we decided to make him the third equity holder in the company. His contributions and positive nature made me want to succeed even more so I could ensure his shares were worth the effort he had given to our company.

Our first hiring misstep came when we were looking for someone to manage social media and our blog. Juan found a candidate through eDesk who seemed qualified, but we learned quickly that she was plagiarizing other posts. In fact, it was worse than that because she was stealing material verbatim by simply copying and pasting to our site the material she had found online. I was flabbergasted and immediately fired her. Her replacement, Weena De Vera, was the opposite type of person. She was open to learning and trying out new things, and she performed every task diligently. We knew she was caring and reliable, even though we had never met in person. Her performance spoke for itself.

As our network expanded and people in Austin began to hear about our educational toys, individuals began to approach Plushkies. This was very exciting. Sugandha Jain, who was the director of a children's school in the city, was encouraging about what we were trying to accomplish because she saw the educational value of Plushkies. Our diversity curriculum originated from a seed she had planted when I was invited to conduct a few workshops with her students. The kids were very responsive when I took them on a trip around the world with Plushkies and introduced them to our "World Friends."

The storyline for the workshop came from a friend of almost thirty years who was interested in our company. Hector Martin, I always thought, was an educational genius as well as one of my best friends. A great deal of our content originated in the mind of Hector, whose positive attitude and common sense combined with his interests in teaching and learning. He was a natural educator, and we were fortunate he took an interest in Plushkies. A storyline he had written became the basic structure for our Plushkies book, *A World Adventure*, and he coauthored the narrative in which the Plushky Plane goes around the world meeting friends.

Our network sometimes seemed to unfold and grow in an effortless manner, though I admit that I tried to pull almost anyone I met or spoke with into my Plushkies orbit. I got financial projections from Jason Fernandez, who was a friend from Duke business school, and Jesse Sosa, whom I met at a South by Southwest (SXSW) EDU Conference, helped me record a teachers' video challenge. These were encouraging developments that continued to feed my confidence of success. I slowly began to realize, though, that all the support I was getting had almost nothing to do with sales and was more about friendship.

A few things changed my attitude and led me to feel more positive about our revenue. Austin's Tech Ranch conducted what was referred to as a Campfire event for entrepreneurs to gather, brainstorm, and exchange ideas and advice. I was selected from about seventy participants as the project and person the group was to support. These conversations got me referred to a social and business club called Friends of Peter, founded by an Austin entrepreneur who was said to be one of the most well-connected people in the US.

Peter Strople introduced me to Gayle Reaume, CEO of Moolah U. We were scheduled for a thirty-minute conversation at her apartment, but we talked for three hours. She had dozens of specific and hard questions about Plushkies. I knew I had to find answers, but I also understood there were no easy or practical solutions to the questions she was posing, because I was already confronting dramatically diminishing resources. I confess to being overwhelmed; I wasn't interested in solving small problems. I had big ones in front of me, and they needed to be addressed and not just talked about.

Peter gave me another name: Michael Strong, a popular Austin educator and entrepreneur who taught about startups and business to elementary students. He invited me to present to his entrepreneurship class several times, and I was able to recruit a team of young students to my Plushkies sales force. As minor as that might appear from the outside, those were very bright kids, and their education was far more evolved than the one I had received at the same age. I hoped their precocious intellect and entrepreneurial spirits might be of some service to my company's growth, and they indeed surprised me with some sales.

Gian Scozzaro, whose child attended an international

school called Magellan, saw my presentation at a pitching competition and told me he was thrilled by the concept of Plushkies and their potential for educational benefit. We later met to discuss how he might help with the product launch, and I was invited to present at Magellan, which led to more great work, learning, and interaction with very intelligent young students. The video footage of that later became a key component of our Plushkies book's Kickstarter campaign.

My optimism, in retrospect, was understandable. It felt like there was great synergy occurring, and relationships and ideas were coming together because of enthusiasm for the product. Plushkies felt like it was coming into existence almost on its own. We had built, very quickly, what I perceived to be a medium-sized company with the operations and logistics in place and ready to scale. Support had materialized in finance, education, and even a bit of marketing. My assumption was that we were bringing into the market a product that people would buy, and that notion was reinforced by all the associates, colleagues, and experts who were lending us a hand for free. We were receiving incredible praise and feedback.

All we needed now was some traction.

SECTION 3

Market (Mis)Fit

chapter 8

Who's This For?

....

THE BIG MOMENT in any startup is when the new product or service starts shipping, beginning its journey into the market-place. Successful companies seem to eventually believe they have figured out best practices that prove their correct thinking regarding shipping and sales.

I know one entrepreneur whose company sold for hundreds of millions of dollars. He was convinced it was specifically the *thirteenth buyer* who proved the value of his idea and led to all the global customers who made him wealthy. Obviously, the magic of his "lucky thirteenth" was merely in his imagination. Things could have stagnated at one hundred customers and then taken off sometime later. He didn't know. I'm not sure most entrepreneurs know *why* sales begin happening or *which* sale was the turning point that led to a successful future.

Whether it was one, thirteen, or one hundred, Juan and I just knew we needed sales. Pressure was mounting on us to find stores to carry our toys and customers to purchase what we had created.

This was clearly our failing. We had concentrated on a linear execution and hadn't thought extensively about sales until we had something to sell. In fact, our sales plan was nonexistent, as was our go-to-market strategy. Our product was done and ready to sell, but it was not selling. We were about to have nine thousand toys in a warehouse near the port of Los Angeles, California, and three thousand toys in another warehouse two hours away from the South of London, UK—and no real customers lined up.

There were other pressures too. Juan's full-time career was taking off, and we were on the verge of discovering how hard it was going to be for him to devote enough time to our project. One day he called to tell me about an exciting opportunity for him—and an increased risk for Plushkies as a company.

"I think I'm going to be moving to California," Juan said. "I've got an opportunity I can't turn down."

"What is it?" I knew this question didn't matter because it was clear he had already decided, but I was trying to understand how much time and energy his new employer would be demanding of him.

"It's with Apple. A great position. They want me as soon as we can make the move."

"Wow, congratulations. That's really great. I'm happy for you, my friend." Because we had been close for so long, Juan was aware I was thinking about what this meant to Plushkies without my asking the question.

"I don't think it will have a great effect on my

contributions to the company," he said. "I've got the relation-ships with the manufacturers in China, I'm already working remotely, and I'm pretty sure I can manage everything on Zoom and the phone. We should be OK. The time difference will make that part possible."

"Plus, it will be great to have you here in the States," I added. "We can get together more easily to plan and execute and work together. I think that will help the company."

I knew that if *anyone* was capable of relocating, starting a new job, and accelerating our company's growth, it was Juan. I also understood, however, that his family was growing—he and his wife were expecting their second child—and they were his primary responsibility. We both remained optimistic, though, because we were convinced that we had the energy and intellect to make our company grow and thrive, regard-less of circumstances.

As if to reassure me of his commitment, Juan came up with our first marketing initiative to generate sales. We spit-balled multiple ideas, convinced that traction and increasing revenue were in the offing.

First Idea: Create intrigue about Plushkies. We drafted and mailed four anonymous letters with progressively increasing detail about our toys. Working from a list of toy stores we thought might bite on our idea, we targeted shops that stocked and sold plush children's animals. There were dozens, yet we did not get a response from a single store. This was surprising since we had included an inducement. But nobody was interested.

Facebook Ads: We did not spend a lot of money on Facebook advertising but were pleasantly surprised when our Plushkies page quickly acquired thousands of followers. We were also equally stunned when not one of them turned into a purchaser. There was absolutely no correlation between Facebook followers and sales orders. My guess is this did not make us unique among businesses testing the market on Facebook. When I looked at the analytics delivered from our ads, I discovered that 90 percent of our followers were also Britney Spears fans. Dear Facebook, *WTF?*

Google Ads: The money we initially invested in Google search terms was for generic terms such as "plush toys." When there was no return, we iterated and searched for long-tail keywords to better target an audience. The cost was lower, but we still got little to no response, comparable to what we'd experienced with Facebook. And with Google, we didn't even add followers. I suppose it was absurd to think anyone might be searching for "plush toys in the shape of countries."

HubSpot: I was new to inbound marketing, but I was excited about what I thought were its prospects to deliver customers directly to our website. I saw the platform as a fine methodology to attract and engage buyers, and I knew our products would delight them. I devoted much time to creating content and blogging in order to communicate our product's glories to site visitors and improve our SEO, but we still did not get any sales from HubSpot.

Chase Jarvis: Because I was living in Austin, I had

annual exposure to a number of accomplished businesspeople and big thinkers who attended the SXSW Conference each spring. At one of those gatherings, I was introduced to the wildly successful entrepreneur Chase Jarvis, who founded and grew CreativeLive, one of the world's most successful learning platforms. He was also a well-known professional photographer and had helped develop and launch a couple of digital camera models for brand-name manufacturers. I figured he had some ideas to help Plushkies ramp up sales.

The conversation began with a familiar question: "Who is your customer? That's the first thing you need to figure out." Without recognizing it, I suppose this was our dilemma from the outset of our launch, but the simplicity of his question helped to re-center me. I had been doing too many things that did not work, and I realized it was probably time to take a step back and revisit basic assumptions.

I certainly wanted to find our customer and turn my focus to communicating with this entity we'd not yet identified, but I was troubled by the idea that there might be some scientific or exact methodology that would provide us that specific answer. Jarvis inspired me to revisit our customer profile efforts, but there were so many niche markets for our toys that I found it difficult to arrive at a clear final conclusion. The answer did not have to be definitive, but we were working from tiny samples of information about our potential target markets, and it felt at times like reaching for something in the dark.

So I retreated to what I'd already been doing. I redoubled

my efforts to find my customer and searched for partners.

International Schools: There were several international schools in Austin, which was becoming an increasingly diverse city. However, I never did connect with the right person to hear my pitch for Plushkies. In fact, I generally did not reach anyone. I did, finally, get invited to a yearly international toy fair at one of the schools, where I was allowed to set up a booth. I was pleased at the response because, as had usually been the case, my presentation and the product prompted excitement. Unfortunately, the other outcome was also familiar: there were no significant resulting sales.

Design Stores: A few blocks from my first apartment in downtown Austin was a nicely appointed gift and design shop. After we spoke, the owner said he was interested in Plushkies and graciously offered to place them in his store for display. I'm afraid I ended up spending more money in the frozen yogurt shop next door than we earned in selling our toys. I can't remember if we sold one or two units. There were a lot of pricey, eclectic products in the store from around the world and, apparently, none of them sold much either. The design store moved to California—mostly, I was told, because of a lack of foot traffic through the door. I was unable to draw any conclusions about the appeal of our toys based on information about the store's fate.

International Mommy Bloggers: Who could be a better partner or interest group for Plushkies than the growing number of "mommy bloggers" around the world? We found about a dozen with decent followings, several of whom had multiracial children. They all loved Plushkies, and we conducted numerous interviews with them, which they posted on their sites and social media and we cross-posted on our social media and blogs. The moms loved our Plushkies, and we did some collaborations, but they did not appear to have major followings and we saw no real sales from our efforts. I considered the results to be inconclusive because we were generating interest, but that interest did not result in sales.

Amazon: It seemed natural to send a portion of our inventory to Amazon. They would shelve the product, process orders from their website, and ship the Plushkies they sold to buyers. This might have been a game-saving moment if we had been able to effectively deliver traffic to our Amazon page so potential customers could learn about our product line. But this avenue was also unsuccessful, and I received another brutal reminder that we had a marketing problem, especially online.

Toy Stores: There were not a lot of toy stores in Austin. I visited all of them and didn't find a good fit, except for one I'll call Toy World. Other toy stores seemed overwhelming with visual noise and shiny objects of no discernible value. The owner of Toy World, though, was nearly impossible to reach. The store appeared ideal for our products, which meant I was going to persist in my efforts to contact the owner and stock buyer.

I had a breakthrough at Learning Express, a toy store that looked like it might be successful in generating some sales. The owner agreed to let me display Plushkies in the store, but when I came back after a few weeks, there had been no sales. She had placed the toys at what I considered a bad location for foot traffic, which I felt was a huge disadvantage since the store was selling hundreds of toys from the biggest brands in the industry—brands that were spending hundreds of millions of dollars on marketing. I decided that our lack of sales was due to the poor location of our display.

Our failure at Learning Express appeared to be another marketing problem. I went to the owners and begged them to let me set up a stand in their shop. I planned to use my orange trunk for a few hours one afternoon to properly display and sell Plushkies. The trunk, a setup I used to market our product at conventions, was relatively easy to move and attracted attention. I was confident I could sell to people in the store who were already shopping for toys. They loved our story, but no matter how hard I tried, I couldn't sell the Learning Express owner on my idea of spending a Saturday afternoon manning my booth in their store. Not too long after this failure, I noticed the store had gone out of business.

Airport Stores: Getting a product into an airport store is tedious and expensive. You don't just convince the owner of the chain that you have something traveling consumers will want to buy; you must also pay them a fee for placement on their shelves and carefully manage the relationship. Publishers, for instance, spend millions getting their books into airport outlets because it can make the difference in a book becoming a bestseller or ending up on a discount table. The results are perfectly logical since there is a captive market inside the airport, and almost everyone traveling has money to spend, often on discretionary products such as books or souvenirs.

I struggled to find the right person to look at Plushkies as a potential product for an airport store. The small, independent shops were my best chance, but it still took a few years before I was able to land a presence in a San Francisco airport outlet. The manager was reluctant to add to her product line and did not want to take on additional obligations. She agreed on Plushkies when I offered to give them to her for free on the condition that we'd share the revenues. If they did not sell, she had no obligation to return the product.

I did not, unfortunately, have any visibility into how our product was being offered, which left me unable to understand what went wrong. Maybe the manager's lack of interest had an impact. I called every few days, trying to strike a delicate balance between being helpful and offering support, and not being a pest. Putting my product in the hands of a seller two thousand miles away who had conflicting priorities didn't exactly make for a conclusive test of market potential. The airport store experiment was, however, a sales disaster. I decided it would also be foolish to spend money on a pricey airline magazine advertisement.

Successful Brands: There were two plush toy brands that we admired in the market. I previously mentioned UglyDolls and GIANTmicrobes, both financially successful products with a strong brand image. We tried several different channels of communication to contact someone in management at each company in the hopes that we might learn from them and maybe even get some advice. No one ever responded. I thought it might have to do with the fact that it made little to no sense for them to offer help to a company that might, eventually, siphon off some of their market, but maybe they never even listened to our voice messages or read our emails.

Whole Foods Market: My apartment was only a block away from the world headquarters of Whole Foods. I walked past it almost every day and just knew that Plushkies was the type of product that fit their demographic. It wasn't only a food store; they offered various other items to their discerning customers. I talked to a few people at Whole Foods but got no help navigating the buying process. No answer, it turns out, is an answer.

No matter what I tried, nothing seemed to work. The number of times I felt lost was increasing, but I still found reasons to be hopeful. I kept trying things out to see what might stick, but there was never any consistent traction for our product. Part of me realized I was trying to validate the idea, but I had convinced myself that our market already existed. I just had to reach it. How, though, I still wasn't sure.

I paid close attention to the new "lean" methodology that was being adopted by startups. In what was becoming almost a theology for new companies, it used what was called a "lean canvas" upon which to build a plan of execution. A critical element of the lean launch was to experiment. You came up with a hypothesis about your company and its products, and then you tested that hypothesis with various experiments. Initially, I thought that could be fun and productive, but it's intellectually absurd to think you can run experiments based in the real world and operate as if you were in a laboratory. At a minimum, I found that notion to be disingenuous, and, at worst, misleading. My experiments, of course, failed too.

Pushing and Pulling: There are two types of demand that marketers and executives use to sell their products: push and pull. This was one of the first concepts I studied while working on my MBA, and it was clearly very logical.

Pull demand is nothing more than manufacturing products that people are ready to buy (there are customer orders), while push demand entails manufacturing products in anticipation of a future demand (orders are forecasted). When you make something new, you intend to either create new demand or redirect one that already exists. You can also put a product into the marketplace that people want to purchase but simply do not buy because there are other competitive forces at work. I once heard that there are more products trying to enter the market each year than the number of products already in the market. That's the level of competition startups face. It might sound exaggerated, but my experience tells me it is probably true.

I once heard that there are more products trying to enter the market each year than the number of products already in the market.

Elevator Pitch: Every startup must have one of these. It's the brief, one- or two-sentence answer to the question of what your company produces or the problem it solves. I messed around with our pitch and initially came up with "Toys in the shape of countries," which I thought was mentally visual and fun. Not much time passed, though, before I preferred putting the focus on the benefit we provided with our Plushkies. We changed our elevator pitch to "Awakening curiosity in kids about the world." People didn't respond to that description either. Maybe it was too abstract. So we settled on "Raising global children," even though our benefit was much more specific. There wasn't much patience for either of the latter two descriptions, and I had to keep coming back to the original "Toys in the shape of countries," because people wanted to know about our product in approximately two seconds. I ended up saying both things—"what" we did and "how" we did it: "We raise global children through toys in the shape of countries."

Startup or Not? This is a big question, and the answer changes during a company's growth cycle. I really didn't know where we were after all the time and money and energy we had invested. There were moments when we seemed like an established mid-growth company, but we had no real sales to offer as proof. We only had infrastructure for manufacturing, shipping, delivery, and administration. During launch, though, I presented Plushkies as a startup because I thought it might make it easier for people to have sympathy and want to offer support. When that had no effect, I tried for the credibility of positioning us as an established company. By now, you will not be surprised to learn that, too, did not work. I wasn't even sure what we were at that point in the company's existence.

I suppose it is obvious to say that things were not coming together for Plushkies. I kept analyzing, though, and continued to pivot and refine various pieces of the overall endeavor. My experimenting did not stop, either, but sales were not occurring. Yet failure to find a scalable path for sales did not change my commitment. I was always trying to learn what was missing and how I might press the right combination of buttons to prompt the arrival of success.

The sad news for me was that these unfulfilled efforts were affecting Juan's enthusiasm, which I understood. He was one of the most resourceful and intelligent people I'd ever known, but I had to realize there was a limit to his time. In addition to his new job at Apple in California, their second child was due, and he had begun to study for his master's degree. Juan had no choice but to prioritize. The disappointing sales seemed to lessen his attention to our company, and the online marketing activities, which produced little to no results, were very disheartening for him, and he was quickly losing hope.

We had another difficult phone conversation.

"I feel like I've been letting you down," he said. "I'm having trouble delivering on my weekly responsibilities."

"I don't see it as your fault," I said. "You've got a lot going on, and we still haven't figured out this thing with our sales efforts."

"Yeah, that's kind of what I wanted to talk to you about. I just don't have the time or energy to keep this up. I can't keep pouring myself and my money into Plushkies if it isn't going to work."

"Well, OK, but I don't want to give up. I think we need to invest more to make it work. We need to keep on building, Juan. Just move forward. Maybe we can make up for the lack of sales by building not just one product but a line of them."

"*No sé*, Ricardo," he said hesitantly. "We could be close to the end."

I did not think Juan was right about this. I had spoken to hundreds of potential customers about Plushkies, and usually after about a twenty-minute conversation, they understood what we were trying to accomplish. Me doing one-on-one sales was clearly not scalable, though, which meant we needed to build an ecosystem that replaced me and made the entire brand and concept self-explanatory.

Juan wanted an explanation as to why we would make *more* products when the ones we had were not selling, and my thinking was that if we wanted to sell what we already had in inventory, we needed to expand our product line so our toys could tell the company's story by themselves.

I didn't think Juan's perspective was supportable because during my hundreds of face-to-face interactions with customers, I saw that they really liked our product after it was properly explained. Context gave our toys more meaning to potential buyers. My vision included an ecosystem for Plushkies that included video games, a social network, and a book. We needed to build a synergistic medium that would give our toys another platform for promotion and a chance to stand out.

Juan wasn't convinced, but he agreed to deploy more capital when I suggested a change in the equity agreement. Our fifty-fifty startup arrangement became 67 percent my share and 33 percent Juan's. I started covering two-thirds of the Plushkies budget. I understood Juan's situation and felt that he was being patient with the company and with me, given our lack of progress. My savings quickly evaporated in the effort, though, and I had to resort to taking out a line of credit.

Neither our friendship nor business relationship was harmed. We had simply changed course and were now going to be guided mostly by my decisions and constrained resources. I knew what was necessary for success, as did Juan, but we still had not cracked the code for Plushkies.

Our marketing problem was a sales problem. The lack

of sales was a consequence of failed marketing. There's a classic business paradox. The company was still around, running on fumes, but we had not yet answered the basic questions any startup ought to have already resolved: Who were our customers, and how were we going to reach them? Even worse, was it possible that there actually were *no* customers for Plushkies?

chapter 9

More Product,
More Marketing

I WAS STILL not properly managing a conflict a lot of startups face. When you don't have the resources—or patience—to do the research to understand your market, you can find yourself concentrating mostly on building a better product. The problem is, this way of doing things can leave you with a well-executed product *that no one wants.*

We were learning a great deal, and I felt putting that new knowledge into Plushkies was certain to create a product that was more likely to sell. But I still did not know our market and needed clearer validation that we were moving in the right direction. We just didn't have the money to improve both the product and the marketing.

Juan's change of attitude to be less involved made this choice even more challenging. We had been through so much together as friends and business colleagues. When he pulled back from Plushkies, I was forced to spend a lot of time critically thinking about the company and the product.

My respect for my friend was great, and it always will be. But I was able to mostly convince myself that his view of the business was changing because his life situation had been dramatically altered by a new job and another child. Maybe it didn't really have anything to do with the shortcomings of our business.

Nonetheless, Juan did not see the point, he said, in continuing to invest in a project that showed no real signs of success. The experiment, for him, was over.

I, however, was convinced we needed more product development to sell the toy. If Plushkies did not move off the shelves, I figured creating the magical world I had envisioned would better communicate our mission of educating children while providing them with a fun toy. Unfortunately, I knew from education and experience that any startup needs two people to succeed: one who *makes* the product and the other who *sells* the product. One of them—or a third person—needs to be a visionary, too, to make sure the right product is being built for—and sold to—the right customer and have clarity about the long-term strategy of the company.

The history of virtually every company ever established

Any startup needs two people to succeed: one who makes the product and the other who sells the product.

has been built upon sales. Sales have to start, and then they must grow. This was not at the heart of my skill set. I realized that I was a product guy, and without Juan's involvement, I was uncertain of how to sell.

The other thing I knew is that a small company rarely has the capacity to generate new demand. It can, however, take *already existing* demand from other products/niches, and I thought there was plenty of demand for us to grab. I ran with that belief all the way…for better or for worse.

I was a very good salesperson in one-on-one conversations. I could easily talk for an hour about the value of our toys, but that was no way to scale our company and its products. We had, however, gained a lot of positive feedback, which was encouraging and gave me hope we were going to make it as a business. Yet I knew there must be a more efficient way to grow than having a founder lose his voice preaching all day. Pouring out our hearts and good intentions did create some wins, but they looked a bit like a kid's lemonade stand—fun and cute, but with no demonstrated traction.

I wasn't starting a company as a hobby, and I had higher aspirations than a second grader's "pretend" business.

Passion was simply not enough. I knew I needed to create systems to do the work. Channel marketing had to be established, along with online funnels and regular orders coming in from partnerships. I had to ask myself difficult questions. I really didn't know if I was concentrating too much on what I enjoyed, which was building the product, instead of directly addressing our failing sales. Maybe I was in denial because nothing was working for Plushkies.

I was clearly confronting a kind of paradox in the business. The vision for our product and the feedback from customers and potential buyers were terrific, but sales did not match that enthusiasm. I wanted our product—which was apparently quite good—to be even better, as if that might compensate for our unsuccessful marketing. I now realize that focusing on product rather than on sales can be a way of not looking the underlying issues directly in the eye.

There were things I had learned from my visits to toy stores that were valuable to our future as a company. Kids usually want what they see on TV or what their friends have. That's often how they—and adults—connect, playing with the same toys. We could not afford to advertise on television, which prompted me to go back out to different Austin schools and conduct more presentations. My goal was to generate interest in groups of kids, but that proved to be unsustainable and did not provide much return in terms of sales. When talking in front of a classroom, I wasn't talking to just one customer for an hour, but still the students did not seem to go home and tell their parents they wanted a Plushky.

I became more convinced than ever that we needed an app, a tool to create a game or a metaverse for Plushkies. At the very least, I thought an accompanying book would make our toy more engaging and fun. The kids who attended my workshops at school enjoyed the storylines I shared, and I assumed that turning them into actual book narratives would increase interest. Parents would see a context and opportunity to engage with their children in an interactive manner by reading the book and providing a tale for their kids to act out.

I began this effort with a presentation at Austin's Capital Factory, a workspace hub where startups gather to learn from one another and figure out methods to grow. A couple of game developers contacted me a few days later through our website and offered their services to build us a Plushkies app with augmented reality. As appreciative as I was of their foundational work, good apps take a lot of time to create, and our slowly growing ecosystem felt consistently basic and never sufficient. I wanted more, which is probably why I grew our product line to four items—the stuffed toy; the passport; a diversity curriculum with games and activities for schools that was downloadable on our website; and flash cards that showed each character's interests such as favorite food, traditions, and prettiest place in nature.

The flaws in our marketing were quite apparent. We did not make clear the instructions on how or where to get the Plushky passport, except on our blog, which was probably not easy for customers to find. Flash cards didn't pass the simplicity test either; they just weren't properly explained. We didn't even sell them on the website because that effort was such a logistical nightmare in terms of storage and shipment. I had to print them myself when orders arrived.

I still didn't think there was anything wrong with our

core product, though. To me, the real problems were a lack of channel distribution and marketing. My focus remained on the gaps I saw that needed to be filled to make our product offering even more compelling. I continued to think that those improvements, even minor iterations of them, would add to our strengths and offset our weaknesses in marketing.

> *There is nothing more enjoyable about growing a company than creating a product and getting it out the door to buyers. It's all about the sheer satisfaction of seeing my stuff outside in the real world.*

Popular author and marketing expert Seth Godin often talks about "shipping product," which even in the digital world is a delivery of the platform or software tools. In a physical context, I am an entrepreneur who likes to ship product. For me, there is nothing more enjoyable about growing a company than creating a product and getting it out the door to buyers. It's all about the sheer satisfaction of seeing my stuff outside in the real world.

Controlling the process is also rewarding for me. The two things I like the most are the creative side of making well-designed products and shipping them out to the market. I admit to a bias toward building. I do enjoy selling, though, especially when I believe in the product or service I am offering, which, of course, I did with Plushkies. But selling isn't as natural for me, and I lack experience in that area.

The Netflix show *Chef's Table* has always appealed to me, not just for the great food and recipes, but also because of its sensitivity in portraying the chefs' stories. I remember in Season 2 when Chef Grant Achatz was told by his executive chef that none of the guests on the reservation sheet had tried the current menu of their three-star Michelin restaurant, Alinea. The implication was that for the guests, it was all-new and there was no need to go through the complex process of changing the menu. Achatz was unmoved, though, and asked a question that I think is important to all of us entrepreneurs: *"But what about us?"* I saw his response as an indication that it is just as important for the entrepreneur to meet their personal needs as it is to satisfy their customers. Pleasure and self-discovery are every bit as essential to the process as is financial compensation.

It is just as important for the entrepreneur to meet their personal needs as it is to satisfy their customers. Pleasure and self-discovery are every bit as essential to the process as is financial compensation.

My personal pleasure with continually enhancing the Plushkies product line didn't prevent me from coming back to the traction problem. I tried harder to sell, buying books about sales and studying the skills that led to success. I cannot overstate how hard I tried to make sales for the company. I understood our very existence depended on getting people to buy Plushkies.

At one point, I decided to attend a small, private gathering of entrepreneurs. Steve Smolinksy, the roommate I was assigned, had significant startup experience and had grown a few companies. He was spending much of his time as a mentor and consultant to startup companies and entrepreneurs. During a conversation while we were walking the beach, he said something that I think was, initially, evading me in the organization and administration of Plushkies.

"The main role of the entrepreneur during the first year of a company is to be a salesperson," he said. "There is only one person in the company when you have your product together and you are starting to launch, and you have no initial funding. So, in the very first interactions you are a salesperson. You are selling someone to give you money. You are selling a store to test your product. You are selling a web platform that they need to carry your product and that you are a good risk. Every single person you run into is a potential funder, a potential customer, a potential partner."

The hard truth about being an entrepreneur is that, whether it's building or selling, if it's your startup, you can't just rely on other people to build your company. Everyone is busy pushing/advancing their own projects, running their own business, climbing their own corporate ladder, or taking their kids to extracurricular activities. The fact that they like what you do or even genuinely want you to be successful doesn't mean they are going to play any role in filling your bank account. Unless *you* do what needs to be done, it won't get done.

> *Unless* you *do what needs to be done, it won't get done.*

Building wasn't selling Plushkies, but it was what I knew.

I also thought about something my friend David Johnston had said to me: "Nobody ever used a product they never heard of." We had not accomplished the chore of making people aware of our toys, and I kept thinking I needed the product to do the talking for me. Something other than me had to do the selling, and I continued to believe the product simply had to speak louder. There was no other choice, since I had no budget for any of the marketing proposals we had received.

I was still motivated and believed in Plushkies after many months of failing to get traction. Going out day after day to hunt and then come back home empty-handed, however, was getting depressing. As determined as I remained, doubt was beginning to creep up on me.

And nothing is more dangerous to a startup than doubt.

chapter 10

Everybody's Pinball

....

IF MEETINGS WERE a form of currency, I would have had all the money necessary to pay for marketing Plushkies.

I was always meeting with people in coffee shops and over lunches I could not afford, talking to every person I'd ever been connected to who might be able to offer any kind of help. I was respectful of their time and thought long and hard about what I might be able to offer them and how I viewed a possible collaboration. I always knew what I intended to request prior to any meeting, and I wanted to be ready with a proposal the other party would find difficult to reject. Often, a potential partner asked for something, and I exerted extra effort to meet their requests, even though this usually meant the people on my team had to work additional hours to present those specific ideas in actualized form.

Most of these meetings were held at the other party's convenience. While I was trying hard to construct win-win deals with these potential partners, I discovered I was fielding request after request and getting almost nothing in return.

There was no effort from the other side in making things work. This did not stop me from trying to fulfill these requests because I held on to the hope that if we customized our product offering as they had asked, we might develop a mutually fruitful relationship.

Staying focused and on task was also a challenge because I wasn't seeing any traction, and that fed my doubts. I wasn't sure if I was working on the right issues or meeting with the correct people, if I had lost my sense of direction, or if I was just being bounced around.

I was starting to feel like everybody's pinball.

It was not unusual for me to cross what I perceived to be a blurry line between going out of my way to offer a perfect proposal and desperately grabbing any opportunity as if it might be our last. Even though I was fighting doubt that bordered on complete disbelief, I refused to let anything pass before me that might represent a chance to succeed.

I also could not believe how people with whom we were trying to do business could be so mindless and insensitive. Instead of giving us a simple no for an answer, they frequently asked us to deliver more to meet their requirements. I cannot begin to measure the time and resources I wasted on this. I truly believed I was doing what I was supposed to be doing by being open to any and all opportunities to grow Plushkies, but I began to realize I was making decisions from a lack of clear direction.

The result of this flailing was that I lost focus and control of myself, and I went chasing after every shiny object anyone dangled in front of me. There was no person I wouldn't meet and no lead I didn't follow. I never bothered to measure the size of an opportunity and what it might mean for the company. Nothing was too small for me. I was likely to spend an entire weekend at a toy fair just to sell a couple of toys.

Unsurprisingly, I began to feel and look desperate and worn down. I kept believing, though, that if I continued trying new things, something would stick. This led to a new dilemma: I didn't know whether to stick to a plan that wasn't working or to continue chasing other ideas and opportunities. I couldn't even identify what wasn't working. Was it the strategy or my execution that was flawed?

Yes, I struggled with giving up a plan that was getting us nowhere.

My undying enthusiasm for the Plushkies product also caused me to stumble and make a few mistakes. For example, one day I drove to San Antonio, filled with excitement about a toy fair I was attending—until I discovered it was all about comics and superhero memorabilia. Shouldn't I have gotten further details before jumping in the car? After looking around at the scene, I didn't even bother setting up my display booth. I did have a nice lunch down by San Antonio's historic River Walk, though, and some pretty good ice cream.

Another piece of advice I took was to partner with various chambers of commerce. I visited with several in Austin but was drawn to the San Antonio Hispanic Chamber of Commerce because it was the biggest and offered a chance to get our toys in front of the Mexican American population. I thought they would have a natural interest in our US and Mexico Plushkies. I made another trip to sign the agreement with the chamber and finalize a press release that mentioned our toys. However, I learned that sending out a news release without existing brand recognition was a bit like tossing a message in a bottle into the ocean if you were stranded on a deserted island. You might be rescued, but it was unlikely—and you had no control over when it might happen.

But I was in San Antonio again, so I took the time to visit the Alamo.

I wondered if I was ever going to be able to figure out how much weight to give others' ideas about what they thought were good business opportunities. How open was I supposed to be to these concepts, especially when almost everyone had caused me to deviate from my path and had, thus far, taken me nowhere?

People were almost unbelievably disingenuous. Why lead someone to believe you might work with them when it is easier to give them an honest no? When I set up my booth at a conference next to a company I'll call Teacher's Depot, I thought they might be a perfect partner. An Austin-based supply store for teachers, they were in the process of expanding across Texas. A couple of people working their booth seemed impressed by the number of teachers who were expressing an interest in Plushkies and the idea of raising and educating global children. I became acquainted with two staffers for Teacher's Depot and suggested we might be a perfect fit for their product line.

Their response was very enthusiastic, and they told me their CEO and owner, Lisa, was the one who made purchasing decisions. They gave me her contact information and I immediately began sending her emails, asking for an in-person meeting, but I was never able to connect with her or have any kind of a cursory conversation. Instead, I received Lisa's thoughts through the filter of her employees I had met at the conference. They had shown her our toys and she provided feedback, which were modifications or additions she wanted to see before she would consider selling any of our products through Teacher's Depot stores.

We had no budget to make these alterations, but I made the effort because I had confidence in the relationships I had built with the Teacher's Depot key employees. Plus, we just seemed like the right product for their company's customers.

The most challenging of the four changes Lisa wanted was new packaging. We had to design and implement packaging in the form of a "topper," which allowed our toys to be displayed in hanging form precisely as she wanted them in her stores.

Our designer, Bruce Lee, and I contemplated several looks that were attractive and functional. When we were satisfied, I went to Office Depot to have multiple copies produced and then assembled the stiff cardboard pieces and hooks. All requested changes were addressed, and I presented the final product to my employee contact to bring to Lisa, who still would not speak directly with me. I could not help but feel this was odd, since we were both part of the Austin business community and had entrepreneur friends in common.

I didn't have to wait long for Lisa's response. She quickly sent word that there was no room for our toys in her stores. I was flabbergasted. Worse, I was probably closer to the end of my emotional rope than I'd thought. By this time, I'd been jerked around, left hanging, and rejected more times than I could count. Looking back now, I can see the seeds of bitterness and anger that were taking root in my heart and mind.

I'd like to say I had a mature and understanding response to Lisa's rejection. I'd like to say I handled it like a champ and interpreted her answer from a strictly business viewpoint. I'd like to say I wished her well and then moved on to another opportunity with peace in my spirit.

Sadly, none of those things is true.

Instead, I put Lisa through the wringer—at least in my imagination. In the quiet, hidden part of myself, my response sounded more like: *Why the hell would she put us through such a trying exercise just to tell us no? It's not like her product line is any better than what we're offering. They have hundreds of mindless/outdated products in their stores. They only would have benefited from making room for Plushkies.*

And what about at least giving me twenty minutes of her time after I've spent weeks addressing her feedback? My designer

worked long hours without pay to create packaging to her specifi-
cations, and she couldn't spare just a few minutes?

A person in a position of power drained our resources and
then was unwilling to give us the smallest opportunity—or even
treat us with some degree of sincerity.

I've had it!

Sound familiar? My guess is that every entrepreneur has had
a similar inner monologue a time or two after a harsh rejection.

The unpleasant experience made me recall another
episode of my beloved show *Chef's Table* when Enrique Olvera
opened his new restaurant Pujol. Nobody was patronizing his
place even days after the opening. His competition, right next
door, had a line outside and around the building, which hurt
because he knew his food and dining experience were superior.
Enrique thought he might have to close Pujol and said, "It's
the worst feeling on earth."

That's exactly how I felt. I had given my best to create a
product that was new, different, and, I believed, higher quality
than other plush toys on the market, but customers had no
idea and didn't know what they were missing.

I kept trying, though. Everyone couldn't be as incon-
siderate as Lisa. I met with an adoption agency that helped
American families adopt Chinese children, and they really
liked the idea of giving our toys as gifts to Chinese kids when
they met their new American families or when they landed in
the US for the first time. Our initial conversations were energetic and involved an exchange of ideas, and I followed up

I had given my best to create a product that was new, different, and, I believed, higher quality than other plush toys on the market, but customers had no idea and didn't know what they were missing.

after an appropriate period of time. There were enthusiastic responses from the agency initially. However, their delays in returning my calls and emails slowly grew longer until they stopped replying altogether. I again ran the gamut of ideas and emotions when figuring out how to deal with another approaching failure, but I could do nothing other than be charming, wait, suggest, hassle, and follow up, until I ultimately gave up.

I was still not recognizing my own desperation. I was psychologically too wrapped up in my dream and all the associated goals to be conscious of anything subtle. I had to confront the reality that I was putting in a lot of work and that any potential partners, the market, and the world in general were not responding.

I remained convinced of the bigger opportunity, but I should have been more attuned to market signals, and they were starting to sound like a train's long whistle as it approached an intersection.

Everybody's Pinball

I even began to see myself as a boxer, but I was bouncing around the ring, falling into the ropes on one side and then slinging myself across to the other while thinking I just needed to get in one good punch to my opponent's face. But who was I up against? I *still* thought all we needed was a good initial sale that would put us in the game and maybe even generate a domino effect. My vision for Plushkies remained big, but I almost stopped daydreaming about it because my daily endeavors were so all-consuming. I was fixated on the milestone of a good sales contract to create momentum.

I recently heard Jensen Huang, cofounder and CEO of the global manufacturer of high-end GPUs company Nvidia, say that if he had known how difficult it was going to be, he wouldn't have started. In his own words, "that's really the trick of an entrepreneur. You have to get yourself to believe that it's not that hard, because it's way harder than you think."[8]

If an entrepreneur who was able to figure out the challenges and move forward feels like that, imagine how it feels to one who can't seem to find a way to place enough steps in the right direction to gain momentum. Selling only twenty to sixty dollars' worth of your product month after month makes you question everything.

Want a real insight into how desperate I was becoming? A distributor we had met at a toy conference asked us to consider making toys for dogs. For a second, I thought about it, and in retrospect, given how crazy people are for their pets, maybe that would have been a winner.

The harder I tried, the more lost I felt. This is not how I thought I'd run a business. My destiny was in the hands of potential partners or investors who I barely knew and who did not care about me. I was losing control of my business, and worse yet, of myself.

I suppose I was having the experience of many entrepreneurs. They all seemed to face unexpected challenges they were not prepared for. But isn't that part of the process?

When I started, the only scenario I entertained was running a growing business myself. I wanted the excitement of momentum and new opportunities and the fun of building a dream. Instead, I was becoming a desperate man, even defeated, and I was disappointed in all the people who refused to give me a chance. Generally, though, I began to believe I had let myself down.

And I started to wonder if I was approaching the end.

chapter 11

When "No" Is the Norm

....

THE OPTIMIST in me still believed we just needed one big break to save our startup, and that it could happen any day despite our past fiascos.

Everywhere, I had faced rejection, and there was nothing subtle about the way I had been treated. I am not an overly sensitive person and was deeply acquainted with rejection in everything from jobs to sports to women to schools to many things I had tried. Isn't that just part of life? I expected to experience rejection when I became an entrepreneur. What I didn't anticipate was that it was almost clinical and even hostile. There were even a few times when I felt that people were angry I'd even asked them to be involved.

One of the big milestones I had yet to achieve, and one I thought might save the company, was a meeting with the management of a popular Austin toy store, Toy World. They appealed mostly to an upscale market and had several innovative products in their stock. While I had convinced myself they were an ideal partner, getting a meeting with them took a few years. I never understood why it was so difficult to schedule a simple conversation in person, because there was certainly no obligation attached to talking to the Toy World manager.

Maybe it was just my dogged persistence, a quality I admit to possessing, but I finally got a meeting with the Toy World store manager and owner. My purpose and plan were clear to me, and I was completely ready to close a deal when we met at a shoe store, which the manager and owner also owned, next to the toy store.

"The first thing I want to do is thank you for your time," I said. "I know you're busy, but I really believe we have a toy that will sell for you, because your own customers have asked me to put it in your store."

"Yes, I know." She came across as deadpan and distracted, and I knew this was going to be a challenge.

"Just by way of background, I'm an international toy entrepreneur. We started our business here in Austin and have early global distribution."

"OK."

"Before we go any further, let me just show you one of our Plushky toys." I reached over to take a couple of them out of the large bag at my feet, very excited about finally getting our product in front of this reputable businesswoman.

"There's no need," she said.

"I'm sorry?"

"I'm not interested."

"But how can you not be interested? You haven't seen the toys."

"Yes, I have. I looked at them on your website."

"And that's enough for you to decide you're not interested in us? I don't understand."

"I'm sorry. They're just too colorful and too branded. They're not for us."

She stood up and left me sitting alone with a bag of toys in a shoe store. I was almost humiliated by the experience, and I wondered if that was maybe her goal as some sort of retribution for my persistence at asking for a meeting.

I had been looking forward to this opportunity for years, had opened my heart to give her the pitch I'd so carefully prepared, and she wouldn't even let me get started. I had been turned away by yet another potential store before even having a chance to say what I had come to say. I looked at Toy World's inventory and then back at our Plushkies that I thought were so special, and I left completely confused.

I knew business could be brutal, but shouldn't there also be a basic politeness and kindness given to someone just starting out? Consideration of another person's ideas doesn't seem like too much to ask of those who have already made it and might have advice to offer, even if they don't want to partner with you. I suppose I should have gotten a clue from her resistance to meeting with me in the first place, and I wondered if maybe she just agreed to meet in order to get me to stop calling her.

The speed with which I was dispatched by the Toy World owner made me think of a college professor, Dan Ariely—author of the popular book *Predictably Irrational*—I'd had years earlier while attending Duke University. Dan Ariely had given much thought to behavior while he was recovering in an Israeli hospital after being badly burned across his face and body.

I was in his behavioral economics class when he told a story about a decision his nurses had to make when they came in every few days to change his bandages. He explained that there are two ways to pull bandages off a bad burn. You can peel them off slowly, which is less painful but takes much longer—less pain over more time. Or you can pull them off quickly, which is much more painful but relatively quick—more pain over less time. The nurses, wanting to be as gentle as possible, preferred the slow method. Dan preferred having them go quickly just to get it over with.

Maybe that's a version of what happened to me with Toy World. But how could I know since the conversation was so abrupt and curt? I certainly felt no compassion or consideration from that businesswoman—but she didn't owe me any. I got her quick hit of pain, but it seemed to come without the slightest intent of compassion or thought. Instead, it felt arrogant. She made it clear she was acting from a place of power and superiority, and when I left that room, I felt as if I had been bullied.

I admit I was hurt deeply by what transpired in that brief

meeting, but I also knew I was capable of dusting myself off, getting back up, and staying motivated about Plushkies. When you are very close to your venture, you identify more with it and allow yourself to be defined by its status. The entire startup experience can

When you are very close to your venture, you identify more with it and allow yourself to be defined by its status.

become personal, and that can be very harmful if you fail. If I had witnessed this happen to anyone else, I'd have been equally flabbergasted. My eyes were certainly opened even wider on my entrepreneurial journey as I realized more clearly the types of people I could expect to encounter as I tried to bring my company into the world.

I had never even contemplated this kind of thorough, relentless rejection as a possibility. It seemed almost abusive. As I mentioned, I was no stranger to rejection in my personal, academic, and professional lives, and I had been treated unfairly multiple times, but I had never encountered such disrespect. I knew the statistics and understood how hard it was to become a successful entrepreneur, but I figured failure was a product of plans and ideas not working or tough competition from a better product or one that had more effective marketing. I had never really contemplated that I might confront dismissive and even abusive attitudes.

But they kept coming.

A connection from Duke introduced me to one of the founders of a multinational toy company. When I looked at their story and their motivation, I thought once more I had found an ideal partner. They had been in business for almost a quarter century, were making useful and educational toys, and were succeeding financially by building a great reputation. The mutual friend this businesswoman and I shared through Duke gave us a very warm and enthusiastic introduction, and he said she wanted to help both of us with our businesses.

It didn't work out, though. I sent her several emails asking for just a few minutes of her time for feedback and advice. I never saw a response. And so I stopped trying. I really didn't get this one, because I came to her well-recommended, she knew my industry, and we had attended the same university.

I wish she'd just communicated back through our mutual friend that she wasn't interested. It would have saved me time and energy that I could have spent on other, more fruitful leads. Plus, adding some human caring would have mitigated my disappointment.

Although I'm not sure how, I maintained my fearlessness. I hadn't expected any of those rejections, and even though they were now becoming the norm, I disregarded more missed opportunities as outliers.

Nothing was working, but I kept pitching my product, again and again and again. I continued to refine my presentation and my messaging. I was motivated by an unfailing conviction in the inevitability of success. Every time I was told, "No thanks," I pulled myself up emotionally and physically and got back to work. The irony was that my determination to succeed just kept leading me to more rejection. I couldn't deny, though, that I was beginning to feel the cumulative effect of the pain.

What if I was destroying myself while trying to build a startup?

I kept pitching my product, again and again and again. I continued to refine my presentation and my messaging. I was motivated by an unfailing conviction in the inevitability of success.

chapter 12

Eating Rejection
for Breakfast

ENTREPRENEURS NEED to follow leads.

Then we follow leads of leads that lead to other leads that more often than not lead nowhere.

Through this agonizing process, I discovered I was connected to a couple of international distributors. We arranged a meeting at their office, which, oddly enough, also doubled as a storage unit.

I was still searching for partners. Getting access remained difficult, and most either didn't want to talk to the founder of a startup or were skilled at avoiding risk. They usually had a list of requirements and financial demands. If they felt they were in a great position of strength in negotiations, they insisted on a significant cut of revenues, even though almost no work was expected of them. We just needed them to plug our product into their existing sales channels.

That's not what I was looking for. I wanted depth and growth potential from strategic partners. They needed to be

The ideal partner would be someone who grasped our vision; they would easily get what we were about and would contribute smart, innovative ideas to help us acquire customers.

willing to work together to build our brand, which would lead to the benefit of abundant sales for both parties. The ideal partner would be someone who grasped our vision; they would easily get what we were about and would contribute smart, innovative ideas to help us acquire customers. I wanted partners who saw Plushkies through my eyes and imagination.

But I just could not make that happen.

The storage facility meeting had no glory to it, as might be expected. The potential partners wanted me to ship Plushkies to various countries to be warehoused. Their end of the deal would be to take and fulfill orders. Easy money, and they had no intention of marketing. How would anyone know to order one of our toys? They gave an obscure explanation for their approach, which offered no logic: "If it's on a wall, it's not going to call attention to itself, and it's not going to sell."

Huh?

I guess they assumed our toys would go unnoticed on a wall or shelf in a store. They mentioned some shiny object they had sold that had done very well for them during the Christmas season because it had an unusual function or characteristic, but my attention span was waning, and it was getting harder to listen. Their approach ran counter to an emerging trend in marketing that I was beginning to find fascinating. Brands were becoming more subtle and reinventing themselves by taking greater care in product presentation. Even basic items such as socks were being redesigned as interesting consumer products.

I told the storage facility guys about Bombas socks and how they were building their brand. A sock is a mundane object, but when I saw a video by Bombas that showed their attention to detail and dedication to improving their product, I decided to contribute to their Kickstarter campaign. Bombas socks wouldn't "call attention to themselves" if they were hanging on a display alongside two hundred other pairs of socks, but their video made it clear they were a unique offering.

I couldn't resist their marketing. I bought a bunch of Bombas and elevated my sock game.

I wanted people to see Plushkies in the same unique, considered perspective. We might look like another toy from a distance, perhaps, but there was much more about our product that parents and kids could appreciate when they took the time to consider what we were offering. Unfortunately, I discovered that prospective partners had no interest in doing the work to get involved in the marketing of our product— especially not in educating the consumer about the window to the world our toys provided.

Bombas brought to my attention a marketing idea referred to as "movement," which is an effort to reinvent a traditional and long-ignored or forgotten product. In too many cases, this includes ridiculous levels of fact distortion just to sell the product. Parodies of "movement" are all over the Internet, including one that shows how to reinvent a bowl.

These types of twists lead entrepreneurs to claim they've developed "the Uber of dog poop pickup tools to make the world a better place." Sure, I'll get the app, and you can pick up my Fido, hustle him to the dog park, get pics of him pooping so I can be sure I get my money's worth, and then hurry him back to me.

I concluded that everyone wants a product that is going to sell itself, and I didn't have one.

The Imaginarium might have come close. I got an introduction to this global company through friends of my parents who happened to be connected to its founder.

I *really* wanted them to add my product to their inventory. They were an unconventional toy store and talked about "solutions to educate in values and support the personal growth of children." Their central goal was to create toys to "enhance the talent of little ones." It was like their purpose was, in many ways, written with my product in mind. Even better, the Imaginarium was in twenty-eight countries and had more than 360 physical stores.

Not only was their mission one that comported with Plushkies, but they were headquartered in my hometown of

Zaragoza, Spain. They were a modern, international store chain with outlets in major cities and even airports, and they were looking for creative toys. I was really excited by the prospect of this partnership and could not wait to meet with the CEO on my next trip home.

When I finally got to sit down with the CEO at the headquarters in Zaragoza, he was completely unimpressed and disinterested. He said they carried their own toys in our category and had no interest in partnering with or helping us in any manner. I persisted and brought up several ideas, such as a small marketing test in one of his stores.

Every option I brought up turned into another rejection. It was hard to finally meet, through a very warm connection, what I thought was the perfect partner and leave the meeting feeling no reciprocity on their part—not even a referral to another possible lead.

Another friend referred me to the company Little Passports, which introduces children to geography, travel, and world cultures through monthly subscription boxes and which was doing well with its innovative concept. I did my usual outreach, emailing and calling—several times—to introduce our company and explore potential partnerships. They might as well have given me one of their Little Passports to go away and leave them alone. Never heard a word back from them.

My luck wasn't much different with investors, either, which I was painfully reminded of one bright, sunny Austin morning. After speaking with Hussayn, one of our most important advisors, I put together what he and I felt was a strong business plan and investment proposition. I then was introduced to Raj, an Indian American businessman in Austin, who was willing to hear my presentation. I think it might be going too far to suggest he was interested, though. Raj was quite generous with his time and listened for two hours as I detailed every iteration of our product development, milestones achieved, and vision for the company.

And then I got to the big moment: the ask.

"So," I said, "as you can see, we have built an airplane. Now we just need the resources to get it into the air and make it fly."

I'm not sure the entire sentence was out of my mouth before he interjected a response. "That's not an airplane," Raj said. "It's more like a part of the landing gear. Maybe a wheel."

This statement was hard to swallow. Raj was clearly a helpful person and had just given me most of his morning to hear about my young company. He had been asking sincere questions and offering wise feedback throughout my talk. He was patient and kind, which made me think, perhaps, he might invest a little money. I was wrong.

"I suppose there is some truth to your assessment," I argued. "But I think we can finish the plane and get it to fly with some help. Any chance I can get you to invest?"

"I'm sorry. I'm just not an investor for this. I'm afraid I have to pass."

There are moments in an entrepreneur's life when you get

the feeling you are living in a parallel reality. You wonder, *Why am I the only one who can see this?* The success of the product seems so obvious to you that you wonder how you're failing to communicate its obvious value to others. But I knew that was not the case for how I was selling Plushkies. My presentations were filled with detailed information and my passion for the product. Yet they failed to attract any investors or partners.

I began to feel like too many of my days started with rejection as the unrequested hot sauce on my breakfast tacos.

Investors often used kid gloves to tell me no, but their answers were just as distinct and definitive as partners who took a pass. There were times when I received interest and a request for follow-up information as a possible investor did a bit of due diligence, but no venture capitalist put even one dollar into my company.

There's an overworked cliché in business that has been around for many decades, but maybe it's lasted because it has more than a germ of truth to it: "If you want money, ask for advice. If you want advice, ask for money."

Maybe I needed to spend more time seeking advice, because none of my little tricks or sayings were working—not with investors, not with partners, and not with customers. I learned quickly, too, that almost no one wants to be the first to put in money, nor do they want to do it alone. Risk almost always must be shared. They want successful partner investors to jump into the pool too. Venture capitalists I encountered were very risk-averse, relied on never-ending due diligence, and responded to a herd mentality. Their biggest motivation often looked like it was little more than a fear of missing out, which they did not experience until they saw that one of their buddies or contemporaries had put money into a project.

The angel networks were the worst of these investors. They were local associations of investors who usually got the first shot at business pitches. My sense was that they were a membership made up of people who were afraid of a party taking place while they were looking in through an outside window. They felt more like a social club than an investment organization.

I was, unfortunately, a naïve, neophyte entrepreneur with a misplaced concept of angel investors. I had an idea of how they should be spoken to and thought about in terms of changing the lives of startup companies and visionaries. I thought these successful and fortunate people with capital resources might wake up on the right side of the bed, snap their fingers, and change my life and grow my company.

It never, ever works like that, though.

One of the final, annoying insults in my search for investment capital was the constant refrain from people that I needed to get on the television show *Shark Tank*. I cannot count the number of times I heard this from people who heard my Plushkies pitch. The reality show was on network TV and featured entrepreneurs pitching their young companies to a panel of investors, any one of whom could offer to put money into the startup or even buy it out completely. I had tried almost everything else, so why not take a shot at this improbability?

I called, left messages, and sent a few emails to the show, expecting nothing after my previous experience with investors. Surprisingly, they responded, which led to a phone interview. Everything was going well until I was asked about my revenues, and that ended my television career.

Even friends could find a way to distance themselves from what I was trying to do with Plushkies. I met a fellow alum from Duke in Austin, who I thought was quite smart, and we became friends. When he heard about my company and my attempts at landing investors, he mentioned that his brother, a successful ophthalmologist, was constantly approached with pitches. Still relentlessly optimistic, I impulsively suggested that my friend and I have lunch, where I proposed that we get his brother to invest in Plushkies and the two "Dukies" could run the company. I am inclined to think my friend was not offended, but we didn't interact much after my proposal.

My belief in Plushkies as a company was unbroken, though—not even fractured—until Raj blew up my airplane analogy. My confidence fell even more as friends to whom I had pitched my product began to "ghost" me. Even though nothing was working, I felt like I needed just one stroke of luck and we'd be on our way to greatness. I had a hard time believing my product was the problem. We had developed a wonderful toy. Why wasn't it selling?

I could not solve the chicken-and-egg problem.

Remember applying for your first job and constantly hearing, "You need experience to get a job, but you need a job to get experience"? That was my conundrum for sales. I needed help with sales, but to get that help, I had to make some sales.

My situation, I confess, was getting worse. I was running out of money and patience, and even the optimism I had once believed to be limitless was beginning to falter.

Fighting for Survival

chapter 13

Windows of Perception

··

AFTER BEGINNING to invest in cryptocurrencies, as I'll share
more about in later pages, I developed a notion I called the
"lower low law." I realized that no matter how high the price
of a coin might be, it could always rise higher, and, as recent
history has shown, no matter how low the price might be, it
can also get lower. There's always a higher high and a lower
low. Sadly, that lower low part also applies to rejection.

I don't want to leave the impression that I am obsessed
with being rejected, but I do think it is important for entrepreneurs to understand how much it can become a part of our
business lives. Rejection (to what you are building) can feel
very personal when what you are building is very personal.
And a startup is certainly personal if we care about it deeply,
and it's about something deeply care about. Which is usually
the case.

I found that, for me, the criticism I received was not
just about the potential or execution of my startup but rather,
it grew from a misunderstanding of the values I wanted to

inspire with my products. People seemed to draw erroneous conclusions from their distorted perceptions of Plushkies and our mission.

In my most optimistic view, I considered some of these unsolicited rejections. Angered, I wanted to respond with, "What the heck are you talking about? This is nuts, and I can't believe I am hearing this. But I guess I'll listen so I know what to expect from anyone else who has the same crazy notion."

Kind of a rant, I know, but that's the emotional spillage generated by some of the comments I heard.

I tried very hard to understand. In their book *Grandstanding: The Use and Abuse of Moral Talk*, philosophers Justin Tosi and Brandon Warmke refer to these types of criticisms and exchanges as "ramping up." They observe, "Moral talk often devolves into a moral arms race, where people make increasingly strong claims, trying to outdo one another to be morally impressive, to signal that they are more attuned to matters of justice." Consequently, this "creates a spiral such that each person competes in a moral grandstanding contest."[9]

I offer that analysis because I was accused of being a racist. The attack wasn't even an implication and instead was delivered as an accusation. One of our Plushky characters, Pepe, was a Mexican and a taxi driver. During the SXSW educational sessions in Austin, I met a teacher who liked our concept and approach to bringing cultural awareness to kids but said that making Pepe a taxi driver was problematic. She wanted to know, "Why isn't he a doctor or lawyer?" I didn't have a more articulate answer than to say, "Because he is not. He is a taxi driver."

Her being personally offended by the description was not my problem. She had the problem with Pepe, not me. I loved the guy. However, when my educational toy cannot be in some schools because one of the characters is a taxi driver, then that is clearly my problem.

I suddenly had the sense that my career and the commercial prospects of my company might be jeopardized by misguided perceptions of one of our toys. I ought to have been ready with a better answer, but I had not thought beyond the hurt.

Pepe, I should have explained, was inspired by my second trip to Mexico. On my return to the airport, I was driven by a taxi operator whom I found fascinating and very inspiring. He spoke to me of his philosophy and worldviews and left me deeply impressed. In probably every culture and economy on the planet, there are people like that taxi driver who are educated and accomplished but don't have a role that's traditionally associated with those qualities.

When traveling the world these days, I often make video recordings of the stories taxi and Uber drivers share with me. I had begun those recordings many years earlier because I loved the local insights from drivers, and I had learned much from the hobby. I never begin a ride with the intention of recording, but I often hear something that catches my attention, causing me to pull out my phone and ask the driver for permission to record their words. Eventually, I will curate those videos, which are stored on old phones and computers, and post them on YouTube for others to see the abundant intellect and personality of people like that specific driver who inspired my Pepe character.

Perhaps I am being overly defensive, but I lost the opportunity to sell Plushkies to a school district in California because one teacher suggested I and my products were racist. That takes the situation beyond just being a hurtful insult. If I preferred apples over oranges, I felt like that teacher might ask me why I hated oranges while also ignoring bananas and discriminating against watermelons. This is the oversimplified way some people parse language and hear words and thoughts. They tend to project confusion into conversations. Why would buying a toy whose character is a taxi driver create a career risk for that teacher in her California school?

That's the world we live in. Even if the teacher may agree that the idea of Pepe being a taxi driver wasn't racist, just the fear of being labeled a racist was sufficient for her to pass on getting involved in a project she otherwise admired. Sometimes people in your industry may want to associate with you for the wrong reasons and other times they may not want to for the wrong reasons.

While it is true that I personally don't want to be a taxi driver, I also don't want to be a doctor or a lawyer, but those choices do not make me a racist. Plus, I find watermelons very refreshing.

Windows of Perception

There is racism in the world, but naming a toy *Pepe* after a Mexican taxi driver is not an example of it. The lack of clarity in our era's thinking truly worries me. Our "windows of perception" appear to be covered in dust or mud. In the spiritual system I practice, we frequently refer to the window of perception because it works as a construct to define the various filters used to view the outside world. People naturally add distorted layers and meanings to external events that are not a part of reality. We filter reality through our view of the world and end up believing that what we see through that filter is reality.

As the old saying goes, "We don't see things as they are; we see things as *we* are."

Our fearful and confused societies are learning to react by labeling and pointing fingers. Sensibility and clarity come from seeking a true understanding of intention and nuance. I confess to being baffled at how easily everyone is offended in our era. How does anyone acquire understanding when they are completely lost in their own personal insanities and disconnected from their own hearts? We don't need individuals who feel morally superior just because they cannot distinguish apples from oranges; sorry, blueberries, for not using you in my analogy, but I don't hate you. (In fact, nobody does.) I think people are completely unaware that they are becoming full of judgment that prompts them to try to change others with a total lack of self-awareness.

We've learned to be nice to make other people feel good and to protect them from what we might think is wrong. The goal seems to be to help them avoid their own emotions of fear and pain. How do we learn without some hurt, though? I think the pursuit to make others feel good helps us avoid our own feelings and take responsibility for ourselves. We spend far too much time trying to justify or assign blame, and that creates victims. People easily take offense but are often clueless as to why they react a certain way, because they are disconnected from their own internal processes.

"I'm a victim. It's your fault. And you need to act in a certain way to make me feel better."

I'm not only saying that we should all be responsible for what we do and say, but we also need to be self-aware and understand our own prejudices and the experiences that might lead us to certain emotional reactions.

I think we are being prejudicial by protecting children from the experiences of the taxi driver. Our adult prejudices are what harm kids, and we should avoid exposing them to our unfounded perceptions. Our biased minds take us so deep into our mental dirt that we are not even aware we are suffocating. The circular motion that inhibits us from accessing the truth is that we protect others from our personal prejudices while also needing them to act in a specific manner that doesn't trigger our negative responses. I can't think of a better recipe to create a crazy world than trying to control how others act so we can feel a certain way and then controlling how we act so others will achieve a certain emotional response. All this while not being in tune with what's happening within us, the origin of such charade. A wall will be erected between our deep inner joy and innocence and our minds by such behavior.

I was affected by the name-calling. My product—and as an entrepreneur, my life—was now in the public. Leaving a big office and going out on your own puts your work out into the world to be judged. This was the first time in my life that my creations or work products were exposed and connected to my name. No longer was I being assessed by Excel spreadsheets and PowerPoints stored in my computer's memory. Even with limited sales success, children all over the world were playing with and learning from our Plushky toys. We had put a unique product into the global marketplace. Reactions were certain to be varied, which comes with exposure.

I can't think of a better recipe to create a crazy world than trying to control how others act so we can feel a certain way and then controlling how we act so others will achieve a certain emotional response.

There's no reason I should not have been learning. I was young, but it was still a harsh lesson to absorb that even when you apply detail and care to every facet of your product and character, you can still be called a word that is the opposite of what you set out to inspire.

The very purpose of Plushkies was the precise opposite of the definition of racism. My work and person were being judged wrongly. Entrepreneurs, I learned, ought not be surprised if the effort they hold most dear, a product built with innocence and purity, is harshly judged by the inadequate minds of critics. If you are affected, though, use the hurt to look inside yourself and take the responsibility that others shun.

The criticisms, for me, were a total blind spot. I had to ask myself how I could have been so naïve, but I gave some thought to how the taxi driver situation might have been addressed. We might have fixed it with money. I don't know what that price might have been, but it was certainly a figure greater than anything our company could manage. To update the booklets that came with the toys, I would have to again work with the designer to change the copy. The booklets would also need to be reprinted, which could no longer happen in China, since the toys were in warehouses in LA and London. The new booklets would need to be shipped to the warehouses, and then the hardest and most expensive part of the operation would involve opening all of our ten-unit cardboard boxes and each of the three thousand individual plastic bags that contained the taxi driver story. A person we didn't know would have to be relied upon to put the new booklet into a new plastic bag and then stitch it to the Mexican taxi driver toy, a thousand miles away from any supervision or direct guidance.

Windows of Perception

Just thinking about the possibility of this logistical nightmare gave me a headache. Of course, it could have been worked out if I had put all of my budget, energy, and focus on the project. That didn't seem to be the wisest use of company resources, though. The best move would be to make the change when we began a second manufacturing round. Until then, I'd have to live with being labeled a racist. Startups tend to stumble, and maybe I failed by missing a possible interpretation of one of our toys. If I had been aware of this flaw in how our Mexican taxi driver toy would be perceived, it is the one thing I would have changed about our Plushky toys. But it was just one more thing I didn't know.

And I didn't think I had much more time for learning.

chapter 14

Breaking Down

....

THERE IS PROBABLY some truth that, when we are emotionally down, every interaction looks like another problem or setback or insult. I was still trying to socialize and go out on dates, but even that sometimes turned hurtful.

I went to dinner with a woman I met through mutual friends, and her only two topics of conversation were religion and the font on my Plushkies website. Seriously, she said it was critical that I get the right font and size, and she offered advice on making the transition. I hadn't conducted research on the hundreds of available fonts, which meant I had no way to know if I had selected the best one for our company and products, but how can you even know with any confidence what is right? I had worked with developers and designers to build our site, and their choice seemed fine to me.

I suppose it's reasonable to assume there might have been a more eye-pleasing font, but I was not interested in redoing that minor element. I needed to be moving forward, not entangling myself or the company in someone else's priorities. My date for that evening, however, insisted I change my priorities, and in her mind, the font was an obvious issue that needed immediate correction.

I tried to turn the conversation back to religion, because I figured even that complex topic would drain me less than a discussion of website fonts. If I had left in the middle of our dinner to change the font on the Plushkies' home page, I suspect I would have made her a very happy woman. She might have even proposed marriage.

But I did not. Our dinner date was at one of those healthy Austin restaurants with fixed menus and prices, and we were at the table only half an hour. I tried to get her to eat rather than talk about my font and her god, and since our date was short, it felt courteous to stop at a wine bar, which was where I found out she didn't drink. I didn't end up changing my font, but I did find different dinner dates.

Plushkies had increased my profile in my small world. Entrepreneurs are often judged more by their company and product, which is what the public gets to see, than they are by their character and personality. Thoughtful suggestions increased in number from my friends and family, as support was offered and comments were made about how they thought my endeavor was "a cool thing." I understood that people saw me as the only reason the company existed and that I was accountable for the site and products, but I had trouble adjusting to the fact I was always going to be exposed and would rarely get a break from Plushkies.

There was no escape from comments and criticisms. Sarcastic jokes were not rare, even from family. One of my brothers, whom I love, asked me in the middle of a big family Christmas meal about the state of my business, even though he already knew the answer.

"So, have you sold a lot of Plushkies?" he asked. He knew sales weren't exactly

Entrepreneurs are often judged more by their company and product, which is what the public gets to see, than they are by their character and personality.

booming. The slight, intended as a minor insult, made me think about people who don't follow their hearts but still manage to have wisdom and jokes to offer to those who do chase their dreams. I understood that most criticisms were well-intentioned, but I was at a loss how to help others respect my dreams if they did not honor their own.

For an entrepreneur, everyone seems to have what they think is an informed opinion on your project. Free advice for your next move. "You should be selling in airports." Oh, really. Gosh, wish I'd thought of that. I processed these encounters in a stoic fashion, but there were times, admittedly, that I wanted to scream.

Unexpectedly, I found that good friends often wanted to have conversations with me about their own entrepreneurial ideas. Completely unsolicited, I got stories about their hidden dreams, as if my decision to pursue building a business gave them permission to share their own ideas. That was an enjoyable distraction for me.

Honestly, though, I was starting to break down.

Maybe that's an overstatement, but I was becoming aware of how difficult it was to build a company with optimism in the face of the cynical delusions of the wider world. The support I needed was also emotional, not just business help. I realized that, to a certain extent, I had been acting almost like a robot. Same conversations, calls, and meetings—to the point where I was wondering what I was even doing. There was a lot of emotion pent up inside of me, I think, because I had not processed all the rejection. I had not acknowledged what was inside me, and I needed someone to talk to about my emotional state.

I began to address this by finding a business coach, Atul. Atul really liked coaching. He had worked full-time in tech companies but discovered he was best suited for helping others. Our initial sessions focused on examining the feeling I had of being constantly overwhelmed, and the last ten minutes we spent discussing my business. He was not cheap, but I knew the money was being spent on a worthwhile service. I had become frozen by my failures, and I needed someone to help thaw me out.

Atul and I had been introduced randomly when I met him while hanging out with another friend. I wondered later if I had looked a bit broken that day or if he just figured I was in trouble because I was an entrepreneur.

Initially, I was unimpressed with him because the first thing he said was something I'd heard many times and felt like a statement of the obvious: "You need to find what your customers want and provide it in a compelling way."

I didn't say it, but the word in my mind was, *Duh*.

He caught my attention, however, when he said, "It's very hard being an entrepreneur if you don't take care of yourself."

Funny, I had concluded it was hard being fit and healthy when your startup is chewing you away, but I felt as if Atul were speaking directly to me. I had a sense that he got what I was going through and that I had stumbled upon someone who could help me.

And I needed help. A lot of it.

Atul also seemed happy, which was a good sign. He said his passion was helping people live their passions, which almost sounded like a nice advertising slogan. We met at a coffee shop initially, and then we scheduled our first session, which involved spending a few hours going over my finances to determine my "run rate." I realized I was quickly going to go even deeper into the red, because his services were not cheap. I negotiated for a volume discount by purchasing a few dozen sessions in advance.

Working hard and getting nowhere will create emotional baggage. I didn't feel like I knew what was happening to me. I felt heavy and discouraged. At times I had to fight off a listlessness that was a product of being disheartened by all the events in my life. Nothing was working for the company or for me, and I was beginning to wonder if I would succeed in any part of my life. I never thought I'd need a business coach, and I sure hadn't included services for one in my budget, but I required support, so I got out my checkbook and we engaged in dialogue. I was at least functional enough to understand that me being functional was the top priority for my company.

Our sessions generally involved Atul in a black recliner, very comfortable, and me on a couch. I just started talking and letting it all out—venting, I suppose. I tried to explain my confusion and lack of progress and how that was leading to an overwhelming feeling of frustration. This purge felt good. I had figured a coach was a luxury I could not afford on my constrained budget, but after many mornings of doing almost nothing because I was paralyzed by many different emotions, I decided there was no avoiding the fact that I needed some help to bring me back to a life of productivity—or maybe to just get through the next day.

Paying coaches and counselors can feel strange because you eventually feel close to them, and it starts to feel like you are getting billed by friends who are listening to your psychological issues. I really did appreciate Atul's unique insights, though, and his care and concern were genuine.

There appeared to be deep wounds that I needed to confront. Atul suggested I write letters to people close to me to share with them how I felt about important matters. The letters were not meant to be mailed but were to help me articulate my hurts and understand myself with a greater degree of clarity. I found this very challenging, but I also knew it was an exercise I needed to do to improve my attitudes about life, work, and interpersonal relationships. At the end of these sessions, I found I was getting back to feeling normal, and we spent time laying out an action plan for the coming week. However, those rarely worked for more than a couple of days because the circumstances of daily entrepreneurial living intervened.

My relationship with Atul evolved to the point where Juan and I decided we could use his help at a big toy conference in New York City. In exchange for covering his travel and hotel expenses, Atul agreed not to charge us for his professional time.

Due to our limited budget, the three of us shared a room. We were all laser-focused the first few days, but since he was in New York, Atul decided to go out one night to meet friends. He came back to the room very late and didn't exactly jump out of bed the next morning to get ready for the conference. Juan and I were dressed and ready to leave as Atul was just making his way to the shower.

So, we waited. For half an hour. We sat on our beds wondering what could be taking him so long. Unfortunately, his behavior affected my judgment of his character and professionalism. His lack of consideration for Juan and me was not the best way for a team to get pumped before going to a show in New York on a freezing February morning.

How could Atul advise me on dealing with life when he was this tone-deaf to the needs of others? His lack of focus didn't help our relationship, but I thought I still could benefit from his support.

Was babysitting Atul just another thing I had to add to my plate?

chapter 15

Sure, a Sales Team

I CONTINUED to feel battered by the entrepreneurial existence. I had turned my coach, Atul, into a friend, and I suddenly was transitioning my friend Husayn into a counselor. I had met Husayn when a colleague suggested I use his startup to send out PR releases on his global newswire. I thought this was a great idea since my company was international.

We quickly discovered we were both Real Madrid fans. Our scheduled thirty-minute meeting turned into three hours of conversation, and we bonded for life through our love both for the soccer team and entrepreneurship.

Husayn was going through many of the startup dynamics my company was experiencing, and his personal challenges were similar to mine. We still made time, though, for a weekly meeting to talk about our businesses, Real Madrid, investors, and customers.

Even though Husayn was having difficulty closing an investment round, he continued to dedicate a great deal of time to helping me through my problems. His advice gave me confidence in areas where I struggled, he introduced me to key people in the industry, and he remained unfailingly generous with his time. I was near penniless, and he always treated me to coffee and pastries and provided a space where I could relax and let down my guard. We also had a little fun, which I sorely needed.

These sessions didn't do anything for my business, though. Our sales came from my endless hustling and constant communication with potential customers. I never let up. I pushed each conversation as if it were my first call to the buyer. Husayn did provide a good ear for listening and understood what was happening, which gave me a way to offload a bit of stress and get some hope or insight. Those things are invaluable when you have serious doubts about your own company.

Perhaps sensing that I was growing increasingly desperate, Husayn convinced me that I needed a sales team. But how do you hire salespeople when you cannot pay even a base salary before commissions? Husayn said I could do it with no budget just by offering good commissions. I was extremely skeptical about his proposal, but I posted an ad on Craigslist and was contacted by prospects wanting an interview.

I quickly decided on a new hire, who agreed to work strictly on commission and said he thought he knew a few people who might be interested in our Plushkies toys. I set him up with an email account, gave him access to our CRM, and provided him with every piece of our collateral materials.

I think he made a few calls, and when he was unable to close with his contacts, he disappeared.

The outcome was no different with the young guy who was supposed to meet me at the Tech Ranch offices. I couldn't find him, and when I called his number, he didn't pick up. When he finally called back, he said he'd been at Tech Ranch and had left a message on a bulletin board but decided to leave his phone in the car while he was inside interviewing with me. I asked him to please drive back for our one-on-one, but he didn't.

While I was filled with anxiety and struggling to keep my company afloat, I also endured the irony of being viewed as a leader. I had no interest in leading anything or anyone that was not related to the survival of Plushkies. I saw the term *leader* as abstract and academic, even a little grandiose. Leadership outside of my company was a thousand miles from my daily reality and concerns. My motives were focus and survival. I had about as much interest in being a leader as I did in crawling across the desert for weeks. I just wanted to sell some toys, catch a bit of fresh air, and then sell more toys tomorrow than I did today. I was focused on putting a few dollars in the bank to last a week, not on being a leader.

During that time, when someone saw me or even called me a leader, I was almost as surprised as when I had been labeled a racist. I wasn't trying to be anyone's leader, and I was certainly not pretending I fit that role. When I met a girl who told me she wanted to provide leadership coaching for entrepreneurs, my head almost started spinning in disbelief. She was living in the clouds. How could she have any idea what an entrepreneur needed to succeed? Had she ever been part of a startup? Tell a struggling entrepreneur you have a leadership program that could be of interest to them, and I can assure you that almost every one of them will look at you as if you are from Mars.

There are many hard-charging entrepreneurs who actively pursue leadership development, but I would argue that the vast majority would have the Maslow's pyramid of basic entrepreneurship needs covered. When you are running on fumes, you don't have the capacity to ponder the noble pursuits of maturing as a leader.

But maybe founders are leaders.

I started a company because I thought I could make money, create a good product, and have fun. All the struggle and rejection, though, changed my default operating mode from having fun to being almost miserable. Come talk to me about leadership while I am in that state of mind.

Nonetheless, while I was working the streets of Austin and putting myself out there as a salesman and startup entrepreneur, this leadership label began to stick, and I started receiving invitations to speak at events. I gave a talk at the University of Texas, and the student audience was intensely engaged. At the same time, I was being invited to join a panel at the SXSW conference in Austin. I was not trying to be a leader, but others thought I fit the profile.

I was certainly not trying to be a role model. All my energy was being spent trying to survive, not creating exam-

Maybe founders are leaders.

ples of inspiration. There were many positive outcomes I had been hoping to achieve that didn't happen, while other developments, which I did not foresee, unfolded in front of me. I never thought anyone would consider me an inspiring speaker, but I got another invitation to talk to kids at Moolah U and became a "barracuda" for their summer camp, where I assessed their business ideas like a shark on the TV show *Shark Tank*.

I suppose I was being a "leader." In my view, that meant I was working on my company with honesty and listening to my heart about the next steps and right decisions. I was not influencing the masses in any way, of course, but I thought I might be living up to the term I'd learned at the Fuqua School of Business when I was working on my master's and we all talked about "Leaders of Consequence." Maybe I could become an entrepreneur who fit that term.

A true leader, I think, tends to be too busy being a leader to philosophize or worry about what it means to be that kind of person. Or to even realize they are one. They just overflow with leadership qualities as part of who they are.

I don't remember where I read that "happiness is the absence of trying to be happy," but my view of leadership reminds me of that declaration. The essence is in the sincere action rather than the reflection. That is, the essence is in the being.

A true leader, I think, tends to be too busy being a leader to philosophize or worry about what it means to be that kind of person. Or to even realize they are one.

It's not so much acting out the qualities you think a leader ought to have; for me, it was the other way around: I was genuinely acting with integrity, optimism, and generosity—taking risks and caring for my team in the best way I could. I was driven and had a vision. Apparently, that made me a leader.

An important part of being a leader is overcoming obstacles. In fact, it is a critical skill, and I encountered more obstacles than I ever could have predicted. I always kept a Plan B and a Plan C in my pocket. Those are business values, though, and I think leadership includes giving spontaneously without worrying about receiving in return. It also requires having a deep, genuine care for others while pursuing goals and retaining a joy in the process of all your endeavors. I think I had all those qualities.

But I was running out of joy.

I'm pretty sure I'm not qualified to give advice, but I have learned some important lessons from my startup experience. You need to avoid giving a microphone to any voice in your head that tells you that you are not good enough to accomplish your vision, or that you need to succeed to be considered a worthy person or businessperson. Don't believe thoughts of inadequacy, especially when they may seem reasonable or justified. Give your best to yourself and your company; that's all any of us can expect. You will likely be judged, but the healthy thing is to see the gift that's in that criticism for you, disregard the rest, and keep the focus where you want it to be.

The recipe is the same, regardless of whether they call you a leader (positive criticism) or a racist (negative criticism).

chapter 16

Bringing in Legal

MISFORTUNE, AT some point, finds us all.

As I worked to make my startup succeed (or at least give it a chance), I sometimes felt that misfortune had my phone number and email address, and it was thinking about moving in with me. I could not predict what might happen with Plushkies, and I saw no value in trying to focus on all the things that might go wrong. I should have, however, developed a general awareness of what might not go my way. The number of things that went bad for my young business was starting to feel like it was a hundred times more than I might have discerned in advance.

This got me thinking about motorbikes.

I started riding five years ago and still smile at the description that motorcycling is the most fun you can have while wearing clothes. I haven't gotten to that level of pleasure (I doubt I ever will), but I do enjoy riding more than I ever thought possible.

The experience allows you to be focused and meditative.

Your awareness seems to increase, and your surroundings begin to make everything else disappear from your life. While on the bike, I didn't think about loans to repay or sales calls gone lousy. There were potential negative aspects like speeding tickets and accidents, but my mind did not entertain those as much as the enjoyment of the road.

I didn't anticipate the fast pace of new experiences and challenges involved in operating a startup. All I saw were those magical, twisty roads through the Texas Hill Country, and I should have had my eye out for cattle in the road along with distracted drivers.

I guess that's how my brain works and may have been why I didn't anticipate the fast pace of new experiences and challenges involved in operating a startup. All I saw were those magical, twisty roads through the Texas Hill Country, and I should have had my eye out for cattle in the road along with distracted drivers. There were certainly more of those in my startup experience than I ever envisioned. Maybe I should have done a better job of planning, but there is much you cannot foresee. Several years ago, my friend Nacho eyed a promising business opportunity and purchased a parking lot next to an event venue in Buenos Aires, Argentina. The business did great until the city changed traffic directions in the streets around the parking lot. "I did not see that one coming," he admitted with a humble smile.

I made a list of the major challenges I faced. It's not a very fun one, but it's instructive to future entrepreneurs to see how a cascade of failures beyond your control can appear unexpectedly. Your misfortunes may be different, but your inner disappointments could be similar. I hope you have none, but mine were brutal.

1. Faked Out by Fabio: How can you win if customers don't pay you? Our Italian toy was named Fabio, and we thought it a stroke of good fortune when we met an Italian toy store owner with the same name. The toys he ordered were our biggest customer fulfillment at that time, and he planned to sell them on consignment. We paid for the shipping; he paid for nothing. I started sending emails and making phone calls. The few times he responded, his answers were evasive. I created a new email, legal@plushkies.com, from which I wrote to him and hoped he might be intimidated by getting a demand letter from our (nonexistent) legal department. It didn't help. Even the US Embassy in Italy sent Fabio several letters that he chose to ignore. If an institution of the American government couldn't move the guy to decency, I didn't have a chance. I'm still waiting for his check.

2. PR as BS: We were approached at Toy Fair New York by a public relations agent who claimed to be looking for innovative products. When he stopped by our booth, he charmed us with a list of TV shows on which he thought he might be able to place our Plushkies. His convincing narrative was that he worked closely with nationally televised morning shows to bring them new products and ideas for discussion. An idea he pitched to us was to make our US toy a gift for Winter Olympic medalists when they returned from Sochi. Although money was tight and our run rate was about to run out, my optimism got the better of me, and I believed we had just come across our lucky break. I invested in the PR and sent several hundred of our "Katie" Plushkies—our US toy character—to their warehouse to use in promotions. Our bad luck may have been compounded when severe snowstorms precluded a big welcome event for returning Olympians and canceled our promotion. The agent gave our toys away to spectators waiting outside the network broadcast studio and sent us a ten-second video of no promotional value. I demanded the money back but was never able to make further contact with the PR agent.

3. No Partners, Pardner: The SXSW Interactive festival in Austin was always a good event for meeting potential partners. I connected with a Spanish entrepreneur from the Canary Islands who had a mobile app and a gaming company in Miami. He said he had released successful video games. His idea was a game for Plushkies using geolocation technology. I was sold on the idea and was utterly convinced it was the viral element I'd been craving for my company. We had a couple of meetings in Austin, and then he simply disappeared.

4. Web Wrecker's Delight: A New York tech company was recommended to us to update our website to enable customers to buy Plushkies using Bitcoin. Several weeks after we thought the work had been completed, I heard from a CEO colleague that he had made a purchase, but the product had never arrived. I checked and confirmed his purchase and saw that his order had not been fulfilled. I didn't understand. We had set up an efficient automated delivery system, and an order via a website from anywhere in the world was supposed to trigger shipment from the closest warehouse to the destination address. When I then discovered that the developer contractor who did the Bitcoin upgrade managed to break our integrated order processing and delivery software, I demanded he fix it. He took an unenthused stab at the work, gave up, and walked away.

5. Promise Breakers: We were contacted by the organizers of a global event for kids that was held in India around the legacy of Gandhi. Children from all over the world were to attend, and the organizers suggested we donate a few hundred toys to be given away as part of a presentation for our company. Although we didn't have much time to meet their deadline, we thought this was another perfect fit for Plushkies, and we spent the extra money to expedite the shipment of hundreds of our toys to India—something we didn't have a budget for. Unfortunately, various programs ran long, we were told, and the segment to present Plushkies was dropped. The toys were happily given away to participants and onlookers without any meaningful background story. We received a few pictures and no impact.

6. Friends and Failures: An Austin teacher convinced me it might be a good idea to have fellow educators send in videos with ideas on how to use our Plushky toys to help kids learn about the world. I thought this might inspire learning and expand our reach. The only person who submitted a video was my friend Hector, who had coauthored the Plushkies book. A few other entries showed up, but they were not captured on video.

7. Wasted Days and Wasted Nights: I spent hundreds of hours filling out applications to be considered for startup accelerator programs—and I was consistently rejected and provided with no feedback. In one instance, I was specifically encouraged to apply by one of the accelerator's organizers who worked for a group described as "the nation's leading consumer product accelerator." I spent five days of a long-planned vacation during the New Year's holiday preparing my application. I wasn't just rejected; I was ignored after submission. When I asked for feedback from the person who had encouraged me to apply, I got no response.

Bringing in Legal

These are just a few of the disappointments we encountered. I can't even remember the number of times we felt we had finally met the perfect person to affect the trajectory of the company with a partnership or promise to assist. Too many times during my follow-ups, they just became invisible. Sometimes, an honest no can be just as helpful as a yes. At least that way, you knew you were at least considered. But we were often left worse off for even trying to engage with these different opportunities because of the energy and time we flat-out wasted. It felt like we were being nibbled to death by ducks.

Even when I tried to give away a product or service, things would go sideways. I started to think we were cursed.

For example, we created a Plushkies Diversity Curriculum and posted it on our website for parents and teachers to use for free. Providing valuable content at no cost to parents and educators seemed like a nice move for our company. I also printed the diversity curriculum to share with people as a promotional tool and urged them to get the content from our website. Everyone seemed to want the printed version, and meeting that demand was costing us more time and money than we had available. Why didn't they download and print the curriculum themselves? In trying to help potential customers, we instead left some irritated that we didn't help them *enough*.

These are very specific things I could have never predicted before we started. The one lesson I continued to learn was, "We don't know what we don't know."

chapter 17

Bro Savior Turns
Bro Bully

....

HUSTLERS CAN get hustled.

While an entrepreneur is out there trying to create and grow a business, they can run into dishonest people trying to hustle them out of money or opportunity. I had never encountered this in any of my other jobs. Certainly, there were political types who were always trying to climb over their colleagues for career promotions or pay raises, but I had never dealt with blatant dishonesty.

There were times when vendors started with good intentions, but they often seemed to choose the easiest course of action. If what we paid them to achieve ended up requiring more effort than they had anticipated, they unceremoniously walked off the job, which meant they disappeared but kept my money. A few even claimed successes that were not theirs, like the social media contractor who plagiarized third-party content and tried to repurpose it as original, assuming I would not notice.

Worse were the people who lied to our faces. We hired an LA company to market our book's Kickstarter campaign, and I questioned their lack of results. The manager claimed her company's efforts had brought in backers during the previous several days. When I looked at the list of donors she referred to, I discovered they were my brothers, parents, aunts, and very close friends. I was astonished she had the gall to suggest this was the consequence of her work.

These incidents happened often enough that I began to wonder about the general prevalence of dishonesty in business. Where does it come from? Why take such chances lying to a client or customer? What is the underlying fear we are trying to hide?

I assume the cause was desperation caused by insecurity about performance. People are probably less likely to be dishonest when dealing with someone inside their own company since there is great risk of being outed as phony. Ultimately, they might even be reporting to the person who is hearing their lies. These kinds of situations can be rectified a lot faster when they are inside a company's four walls, but dealing with dishonest contractors and vendors presents much harder propositions for settlement, especially when you are a small business.

How much energy is an entrepreneur supposed to spend on fighting these fights? I know it's important to defend yourself and take a proper stance for honesty, but building a company is hard enough without having to waste time fighting with contractors. My business was spread too thin from the beginning. I thought the resources I needed to run Plushkies would very quickly come from revenues, which did not happen.

I also did not accurately anticipate the amount of support or service providers that were going to be essential. Their costs and our dependencies seemed to evade my analyses. I needed help, of course, but had no money to pay for it, so I began to try to work deals for delayed gratification on the part of my vendors. They were usually cooperative, but when the timeline to payment and the amount of work required were both increasing, they left and found clients with better financial resources. I understood, regardless of how much it hurt my company.

I also needed a healthier dose of realism injected into my expectations. I kept hoping magic would happen, because the universe works in mysterious ways, but I expected too much, too often. As I mentioned previously, we did try sending toys to India but had no one on the ground in that country to drive our marketing and delivery efforts and, as a result, there was no real return on the investment.

My starry-eyed dreams were falling apart all over the place, even in my personal life. I remember swiping on the dating app Bumble to read a girl's profile, where she indicated that she did not date entrepreneurs. I was astonished. Why not? We, in my view, worked the hardest, were visionary, and risked the most in a noble pursuit, which we believed

> *Entrepreneurs are people who change the world and build the future. And regardless of whether we end up achieving our goals or not, we are fueled by optimism.*

would eventually make us a ton of money. Entrepreneurs are people who change the world and build the future. And regardless of whether we end up achieving our goals or not, we are fueled by optimism. What could be more intriguing and magnetic than the exuberant enthusiasm of an entrepreneur?

My glamorous point of view was shattered by the realization that we were not all perceived in a positive light. I knew we couldn't all be Steves or Elons, but isn't being honest about what one wants to pursue the most important thing? Of course, most entrepreneurs are not successful, and anyone with a blog or Instagram profile can call themselves a founder, a CEO, or especially a consultant—and too many do.

I thought I'd hit rock bottom—until the day I got pushed around by a drunken bully.

We met sitting next to each other at the bar in a popular burger joint in Austin's booming South Congress district. This guy told me all about his social media company, and he invited me to an event they were sponsoring later that evening.

I suppose we were both selling our companies and our visions, but I was prompted to take him up on his invitation and go to his gathering. The evening concluded with him embracing my optimistic outlook for Plushkies, and we began talking about an agreement in which he would provide marketing and sales services for my startup.

Our first business meeting was at Monkey Nest, a popular coffee spot on the north side of Austin. We hit it off even more than we had in our first conversation and started brainstorming about Plushkies. This was refreshing to me because he immediately started ginning up ideas I had long contemplated. He talked about starting social media accounts for each toy and developing communities around those toys and the countries they represented. The language he used and the creativity he was describing were the first indications I had that I was finally encountering someone who saw what I saw.

I thought he had come along at just the right time to save Plushkies.

The relationship began under a small test contract that delivered social media services. In a matter of days, the first red flag appeared via a very distasteful tweet that did not represent our brand. Suddenly, we had hundreds of followers, who were obviously completely fake. The more we worked together, the more I learned about his company and his personality—and I didn't approve of his bots, his office, or his business model of having a posse of interns doing meaningless work. There was also his blatant lack of seriousness in meetings and a very off-putting "bro" attitude. Professionalism seemed absent from his workplace.

Over the course of the next several weeks, we met multiple times to work out a more comprehensive and longer-term contract, though I was becoming increasingly hesitant. This character, though, seemed to have the ability to infuse a dose of energy into my company, and I had been so constantly defeated that I was running out of confidence to succeed without a boost of horsepower. As annoying and intense as he was in person, I needed his help. We arrived at terms, and he agreed to draw up a contract for our signatures.

He shared the contract with me at a local donut shop. The language of the contract did not appear to reflect our verbal agreements. As I read, I asked him questions about items we had not previously discussed. He was not thrilled by my inquiries, and I was becoming less than enamored by this guy who increasingly seemed like he was trying to pull a fast one on me. Included in the new contract was language that called for a base salary, a sales commission, a percentage of my company, and he wanted ownership of his work. He expected me to pay him to work for a company he would partially own—and *then* receive a commission when he sold a product he owned in perpetuity. The way I saw it, he wanted me to pay him for him to work for himself. I had never heard of such a thing.

His plan to close the deal was a claim that he could sell a few thousand toys to local schools as soon as we hired his company and delivered his shares of Plushkies. The more he persisted on these matters, the more questions I had. His initial eagerness appeared to be turning to anxiety as I had not yet put down my signature. The other problem was that he was drinking, and heavily, which is never a smart move during business negotiations.

Getting drunk as your deal is coming undone can lead to some seriously undesirable outcomes. I saw that the deal was as much about his self-esteem issues as it was about making money. He was growing angry because he was not getting approval and validation from me regarding his proposals in the contract. Everything suddenly seemed to be about his own self-worth and how much he could extract from the company and not about a real partnership. I sure wasn't going to abandon the needs of my startup to make him feel better about himself. That's how the negotiations devolved into anger.

I wondered how I kept ending up in such unpleasant circumstances when all I was trying to do was build a business to make money, create an interesting product, and provide a few jobs. After spending so much time chasing potential partners to schedule appointments and then experiencing rejection, I was suddenly in a position where someone did not want to let me go and was turning to aggressive tactics to work with me. Granted, on his own terms. I was confused when in a menacing tone he told me, "I will never work for anybody else. I will always be the owner of my work."

This meant that if I owned the donut shop we were sitting in, I'd have to give him a percentage of that ownership, and then he would want to make a commission on every donut I sold. Plus, he'd be able to take the donuts with him at his first baby temper tantrum.

This was nuts, and I told him as much, which was where things really broke down. That short, bald, pudgy, drunken bully's next best move was to attempt intimidation, and he began yelling at me right there in the middle of the room.

"You're a nobody!" he screamed. "And you'll stay nobody without me!"

Then he walked over and pushed me, physically touching and shoving me. Maybe this was an elegant and sophisticated methodology for negotiating I had not learned in business school, but I was still shocked. Because I was so desperate, and maybe because he seemed so confident in his own ability, I had been trying very hard to reach an agreement with him, but suddenly things had changed. I was no longer interested in any type of partnership. His violence had grown out of my questions, and I could almost see it bubbling up in him as we talked. I left the place overwhelmed and shocked.

And then I went home and cried.

The experience was instructive, though. My desperation had caused me to ignore all the red flags flying around that guy and our interactions, almost from the beginning. A person more confident of their company's prospects and a more self-respecting entrepreneur would not have entertained the clown as long as I did. My morale was so low regarding Plushkies that I suppose I unconsciously saw him as a kind of savior, an individual with energy and ideas that I fantasized could bring the company to fulfill my coveted vision.

The truth I finally accepted was that I couldn't make my company succeed, and I was so desperate that I began to abandon my principles and compromise with people who I would not have otherwise engaged, like this particular guy who had his personal worth and validation wrapped up in getting my signature on an unfair contract.

However, I did not surrender to the pressure, and the next morning I sent an email to my friend Jason, detailing the conversation and the physical confrontation. His unequivocal response was, "F#*! that guy." I already felt that way, but his affirmation was soothing. I needed to hear that my judgment was right. I took solace in the fact that, even though my company wasn't working out, I was still in control of what I would focus on and who would participate in those efforts, either as a vendor, an employee, or an investor. That's what I was clinging to as the clock ran down on Plushkies—at least, I still held the capacity of choosing who I was going to work with, and if I stayed present and true to myself, nobody could make me do anything I didn't want to do.

I had just been yelled at and physically pushed around by a short, bald, pudgy, drunken bully. Was there any way things could get worse?

I didn't want to know.

SECTION 5

The End

chapter 18

When You've Already Tried X, Y, and Z

....

IN MY FINAL attempt to find a path to success, I went back to my friend and cofounder, Juan. His new life in California was fulfilling his dreams, but I hoped he might jump back into Plushkies with additional effort. In his time away from our venture, he had become little more than an advisor. But this was helpful because I consistently needed someone to bounce ideas off and ask questions of. I felt like I still had the energy to carry our business dream on my back, but I was becoming increasingly uncertain if it was worth lifting.

My inspiration was waning, though. I had watched too many movies about the unsuccessful guy who goes from failure to failure, trying harder and harder, until he gets his lucky break. That's how I saw myself. I just had to keep pushing. The mentality I developed drove me to "try this one more thing" or make myself believe, "If the company doesn't succeed, at least I will be able to sleep at night knowing that I tried X." The trouble came from the realization there was always a Y and

I felt like I still had the energy to carry our business dream on my back, but I was becoming increasingly uncertain if it was worth lifting.

then a Z and even another tactic or two after I ran out of letters of the alphabet.

Maybe, I thought, it was time to try an old-school tactic. We had employed social media, digital advertising, personal and professional connections, in-person visits, references, and introductions in a faltering attempt to grow the company. My sense was that we had contacted many people in the toy industry who were in search of new products and ideas, but we needed one big stroke, a final push to reach our goals. I outlined my goal to Juan in a call.

"You'll probably think this is crazy since we really don't have the money," I said. "But I think we need to go to Nuremberg and New York."

"What? You're serious? The two biggest toy shows in the world? We can't do that."

"We can. And I think it will be worth the risk."

"I don't know," Juan said. "Just seems crazy, given how we keep falling flat on our faces."

"Yes, but if we get nowhere after making this effort, then I suppose we have our final answer about the future of Plushkies, don't we?"

"Yes, yes, I guess." He was quiet for a moment before continuing. "If you want to do that, I can only manage Nuremberg. I just have a lot going on."

"OK. That's great. I don't think I could pull this off without you."

"I can't do any more after this, though. My life is busy, and this is just frustrating."

"I understand."

My initial challenge was conference logistics, and I had no experience with managing those types of details. They included everything from applications and fees to booth locations and shipping products for displays. Meanwhile, I worked very closely with our designer, Bruce, to get toys and displays ready, and his ongoing efforts prompted us to make him a third owner of the company.

My tasks were plentiful. I printed business cards, flyers, and shirts for promotion. Juan and I got special Plushkies hoodies to wear, and I packed a full suitcase with stands for the toys, colored ropes from which to hang T-shirts, and tape and scissors to make things fit together for public view. Juan also brought branded tote bags that had been printed with outlines of his two children's hands. When we ran into a problem with shipping, the landlord of our Airbnb in Nuremberg was able to liberate our toys from customs the day we arrived for the show. Our budget was probably the smallest of the thousands of attendees, but I was able to secure a small booth, decently located, and we hired a part-time assistant.

Regardless of the inevitable message we got from the market, I have **fond memories** of those days at the convention in Germany. They were intense and we worked long hours, but we managed to have a great deal of fun. From the time we walked into the convention hall, Juan and I gave it our very best, and what emerged was a serious effort that was driven by passion and executed with teamwork. The last two days were more casual, but we remained professional and walked the aisles of displays and booths, revisited contacts we had made, and tried a few new approaches to making sales.

In the evenings we went out into the city and wandered around while looking for a place to have dinner. Nuremberg was pretty that time of year, and Juan and I, who had known each other for twenty years now, were unshakable friends, no matter what happened to our business. On our last night, though, I opened up about my frustrations with him and how our work relationship had taken shape.

"I have to be honest with you, Juan," I said. "A lot of this hasn't seemed very fair to me."

"What do you mean?" He looked at me from across the table where we were dining.

"Money is a big part of what bothers me. As you know, you are making a good amount of money in California working for one of the biggest tech companies in the world, and yet you are responsible for only a third of our costs at Plushkies."

"I know, but there's a reason for that. Let me just…"

"I need to finish so you understand my perspective.

We're good friends. I can tell you. I've been frustrated because I've been working full-time for our company, not making any money, but still paying two thirds of our costs. This just isn't sustainable for me."

"OK, I understand. You won't like what I have to say, but here it is: I'm just not excited about the company anymore. I don't have time for it, and I don't want to put any more money into it. I stopped believing Plushkies could make it several months ago."

I was stunned. "I don't get it. Why did you continue to…"

"I kept putting in cash to help support you. But that isn't sustainable, either. Plus, I've taken several days of vacation to come over here to help when I really didn't want to. I just couldn't abandon my friend."

"I'm sorry," I said. "I guess I should have been more aware."

"No, not really. You were focused, and I admire that. Your determination has gotten us this far. But now we need a plan for me to leave the company."

"OK, I see."

This conversation was difficult because it was a mixture of friendship and business. Yet I realized I felt a bit relieved. I was no longer resenting a dear friend and actually had grown even more appreciative of him because of the sacrifices he had made for me and our company. Juan and I had achieved a clarity and understanding that had not previously existed because of distance and lack of communication. I think we actually became better friends after this. I asked him for six more months of support to see what might transpire, and he even agreed to go to the New York conference to conclude his efforts on the part of Plushkies. Whatever happened after those six months, Juan would no longer have either equity in the company or the burden of any expenses. Everything would be on me at that point.

Nothing much changed at the New York conference in terms of advancing the company. We brought our flyers and banners and even an augmented reality app. Two Austin developers had built the app for free and included a few games for users.

While the phone app was cool, it wasn't game-changing. It showed Katie's flash cards (she was our US Plushky toy), and if you put the camera in front of a Katie picture or the physical toy, the app recognized her and she popped up on the screen. This was the functionality available to a startup when all you could afford was taking the developers to lunch a few times and giving them toys and T-shirts. I wanted to pay everyone generously, but the company was not yet at that stage. I told myself, *As soon as we get some traction, we'll be able to complete the app, add our other World Friends, and pay a proper fee for development.*

I never let a lack of sales slow me down. While we were at Toy Fair New York we began promoting a Kickstarter campaign to launch our *Plushkies' Adventure Around the World* book. The feedback I had been getting was that a book was the most feasible addition to our product family, and there were enough requests for it that it made me think it might help sell our product. We worked hard at the toy show, and I was excited by the prospect of some potential partnerships and a decent number of promising sales leads.

We met a distributor from Croatia who was fascinated by our company and wanted to be the business that brought them into his own country. His enthusiasm was such that we thought a deal would quickly take shape, but even though we made several follow-up calls and sent emails, we received no proposals. A vendor from Saudi Arabia also said he loved our project and asked for a customized design for a Saudi Arabian Plushky, which we provided after extensive collaboration with Bruce. The Saudi vendor took several samples of everything for his daughters, but after a few early responses, he also stopped communicating with us.

A big distributor in the United Arab Emirates approached us with an exciting idea. He wanted a Plushky for the Burj Al Arab hotel, the Dubai structure famous for its architecture that looks like a sail—and for being the only *seven-star* hotel in the world. Part of the reason I found this possibility so intriguing was because I had been contemplating the idea of exploring shapes beyond countries. The opportunity was coming along sooner than was ideal, but we decided to engage in the conversation. Making different high-end products of iconic locations and premium tourist entertainment centers had the potential to be a huge revenue source, but for some reason the buyer from Dubai turned his attention elsewhere and we were left disappointed.

The unhappiness was accumulating. A distributor focused on educational products to teach geography through a diverse set of toys spotted us at the New York show and was curious about our products. Obviously, we saw him as a natural partner, so we met for lunch, where he ordered multiple cases of our toys. He needed them boxed in a custom manner, however. His buyers would want eight per container instead of ten, so Juan began to manage the logistics of repacking and paying for labor costs to produce the requested cases. By the time we were ready to ship his eight toy cases, the distributor had lost interest, saying that his customers were not as excited as he had expected. This setback was heartbreaking because I thought we had finally found a distributor who shared our mission. Was geography still being taught only using maps and globes of the Earth?

Brand alignment apparently only mattered to me. I had long been a fan and customer of Putumayo World Music and had a collection of their CDs, which I found to be sensitive and tasteful. Their motto, "Celebrate the World," was, in my mind, just a variation of ours, "Raising Global Children." When I discovered they had a booth at the New York show, I had to compose myself because I was so excited—even a bit starstruck. I worked up my courage to speak with the woman attending the booth and told her what a fan I was of their recordings. I also expressed how glad I was to meet them, and I explained what Plushkies did and described how I wanted to explore opportunities to work together in marketing our products, which I saw as naturally connected. Her interest seemed genuine, and she said she'd talk to the owner of the company.

Exercising my usual dogged determination, I followed up with emails shortly after returning to Texas. The woman's response was that she had not yet had a chance to speak to her employer because the company had been changing offices, but she wanted me to check back in a few days. I did, and when I got no response, I again emailed into the abyss. Tired of being ignored after receiving encouragement and promises, I sent another email, this one mildly aggressive with a spicy dose of frustration. I asked her to give me a simple yes or no about whether they were interested. I think that was the only time in all the years I was pushing Plushkies that I lost my cool with someone. I never heard back from Putumayo World Music.

It was just another sad song.

Our book finally came out, but it was too little and much too late to save the company. The two biggest toy conferences in the world had not yielded a single customer. Juan was disinterested and was on his way out the door, and my conviction was fading too. I also lacked the financial resources to properly market the book.

I decided to stop dreaming about startup success and growing a business.

chapter 19

No Confusion, No Choice

EVEN THOUGH I knew my efforts to save Plushkies were not working, I stayed in the mental trench of "trying to make it" for many years. We were not getting traction, and yet I kept putting in my own money and working hard with my head down. There was no question in my mind that this would continue to be my job until the company was a success. I saw it as only a matter of effort and time. After we succeeded, I could move on to the next thing, and I'd have the resources to make certain that would be a pleasant decision.

I've given a decent amount of thought to what I was doing and why I was doing it. Perhaps I had stayed too long at the party and hadn't noticed that most of the invitees never even showed up. I was still hearing the voices in my head listing all the items left to execute to make Plushkies viable. I considered that I might be haunted by quitting because I might be on the verge of a breakthrough. I certainly did not want to live with that ghost.

But I suppose hanging on was mostly a matter of ego. My mind kept creating a parallel reality of success, but when I took an honest, forensic look at my project, I knew with painful certainty that what I was doing was just not working. Something Mason Hale, the founder of SwimTopia, had said, kept rattling around in my conscience. He warned of the opportunity cost of pouring your heart into a venture that was offering little in return. I went from unquestioning devotion—"I want to work for as long as it takes to make this venture happen"—to, "It's true, there are so many other more productive things I could be doing," and that transition was, finally, lightning quick.

It had been six years since Juan and I had begun brainstorming Plushkies, and here I was, consciously surrendering the dream to the rogues of reality.

I wasn't enjoying it anymore, and I wanted and deserved something different from a life of never-ending struggles. It was neither smart nor healthy to continue operating on what had become my psychological version of automatic pilot. I knew I was capable of succeeding with a product that did not require me to work in isolation but instead with a team that cared greatly about the product and shared the effort. I had no idea what that product might be then, but I knew there were projects out there that would not require me to keep pushing so hard upstream in an attempt to bring something into the world that the world didn't seem to be missing or embracing.

I still thought I had a great idea, but the reality was

that I had not been able to make it happen. My love for Plushkies was nurtured by the small amount of positive feedback I'd received very early on, and I failed to understand why the product demand would not scale. My opportunity costs were more than I could afford. Mostly out of money, I was not interested in incurring more debt. I had slowly begun to admit that my genius idea wasn't going to make it in the world, and that hurt—more than a little. I suppose it's a pain the majority of us entrepreneurs face.

I knew I was capable of succeeding with a product that did not require me to work in isolation but instead with a team that cared greatly about the product and shared the effort.

I, however, had been hooked to an idea and a vision as if they were inevitable. When rejection became the theme of my endeavor, my perspective finally began to shift. Maybe my product wasn't all that great, or perhaps the way I ran my operation wasn't the best. I had to commit at the beginning, though; that's what entrepreneurs do, and besides, I had the inventory costs of two warehouses full of toys. Success doesn't just require commitment, though. I was missing a degree of mental flexibility. I only expressed a certain adaptability if I thought it would take me where I wanted to go, which was limiting and clearly not that flexible.

My personality, I'm afraid, tended to romanticize more than just women. That's an Achilles' heel for entrepreneurs, who need to be visionary yet brutally pragmatic. I thought about how my work ethic compared to my personal life. If I met a hundred women, I might disregard ninety-nine of them for foolish reasons and become obsessed with the one who caught my attention. I would see her as the sole human with whom I could be happy. I needed her. I was certain things would be perfect if only we could be together. I confused being madly in love with my lack of self-worth, and I was willing to do almost anything to be with that special person. There seemed to be something about that woman that convinced me she would be my ideal partner, and I kept falling in love with the idea that we'd live together happily ever after.

Building castles in the sky, I realized, felt like a favorite pastime of mine. It began with romantic love when I was young and it had happened now with my startup, but being an entrepreneur had forced me to mature. I intimately understood, through painful experience, the difference between an inventor and entrepreneur, a founder and a CEO, and I certainly understood the contrast between what makes a good idea and what constitutes a successful company.

A dream—one that I had begun full of joy and hope—had turned into a never-ending struggle. I had always believed in the necessity of sacrifice, but I also required a clear picture of what was to be gained and the amount of time involved. There needs to be a window of time for any sacrificial efforts to achieve goals; that is, one needs to set a clear mark when to call off the sacrifice. I had failed to give myself a deadline and specific metrics to hit, and in doing so, I had probably allowed myself to sprint way past what should have been the finish line.

When you do that, your sacrifice loses meaning and impact. Sacrifice had turned into a lifestyle for me, I'm afraid. I had hoped to become exceptional and instead was spending my days harassing anyone who could remotely help Plushkies gain traction—and I was struggling. Minor victories were my only comfort. I had spent too many days living a life I did not want. Nothing is more important in business—and in life—than being mindful of how much, how long, and for what specific outcome you are sacrificing. And if you kick the can far enough down the road, you risk sacrificing your entire life.

Finally, I was seeking understanding more than revenue and success, and I recalled the words of the Indian mystic Krishnamurti, whom I had heard the spiritual teacher Jeff Foster quote:

If you are trying to decide, that means you are confused. When there is no confusion there is no choice we stop trying to decide with our mind we are not even thinking about the problem, and then suddenly we contact within ourselves this deep knowing. There is like an aha moment and then suddenly we just know what we are going to do. It's not a knowing that comes from the mind. It comes from the belly, it comes from the gut, it comes from presence itself. We just know, there is just this knowing, and in that moment there is actually no choice any more.[10]

I did not have to *try* to decide; I knew I had to follow the inexorable pull of life, though I had no idea where I was being taken with this vision of a product that was toys shaped like countries.

I had also begun to listen more closely to my heart and decided I was no longer going to hold on to a concept that was not working. An idea is just that, an idea, not a mandate or a cross to bear, regardless of how elevated the idea is. Foster, again, summarized it for me: "Joy is full commitment to life, even if it's uncomfortable."[11]

People often have a difficult time distinguishing between the voice in their head and the more intuitive one that guides their heart, which is their true self. The first one is intermingled with ego, but the force of the ego often makes us believe we are following our hearts when, in reality, it's our unconscious needy programming that is playing with us like a puppet. The reality is that most of us will follow our egos off a cliff. I was finally being truly honest with the guy in the mirror. I had started by following my heart, but I lost myself in the battle to save my company. When I came back to who I really was, I realized that quitting was the most logical and honest thing I could do.

That doesn't mean there wasn't pain in the decision. Each act of ending a dream offers hurts that are acute, but I knew this time that what I was doing was correct. I logged onto our website and hid the checkout page.

My startup was dead.

What I Learned, What I Felt, and What I Still Don't Know

chapter 20

One Swipe Away

....

THERE IS A GOOD chance that entrepreneurs have addictive personalities.

We diminish that idea by describing these types of people as "serial entrepreneurs," but there is something addictive about living on the verge of great possibility. We often feel like we are carrying a mystical lottery ticket in our pockets. Struggling is endurable when you think you have the winning ticket, and we all believe in ourselves once we launch. I like to compare this to an athletic contest where you know you trained for the big game. Even though you may be the underdog, you are confident you have the X factor that your opponent lacks and will therefore defy the odds and win.

> *There is something addictive about living on the verge of great possibility.*

We also learn to live with contradicting information.

One morning, I received an email from a potential partner and investor I'd had coffee with a few days earlier. We'd had what I thought was a congenial conversation and shared experiences about our respective startup businesses. His was a bit unusual but was making revenue. He had created a diaper business for the elderly in Japan. I sent a conversational email to follow up, asking if he had any additional thoughts about Plushkies, and was gut punched when I read his response: "What you are doing is a waste of time and money."

Hey, at least he responded. That almost made him exceptional.

The same day, I was at the SXSW EDU Conference in Austin when a woman sitting a few chairs away caught my attention and began yelling my company's name. "Plushkies! Plushkies!" I moved over to talk with her, and she told me she had bought one of our toys six months prior and that her son clung to it every time he went to sleep.

These kinds of responses caused me to live in a state of permanent uncertainty. The unpredictability made things intriguing, but I was also overwhelmed by ambiguity. Too many data inputs were contradictory. The angst from a lack of traction was compounded by confusion and not truly understanding where I ought to spend my time. I was receiving too many mixed messages, and it was hard for me to reach a final conclusion and define a clear direction. The solutions to my problems were out in the real world and not two cubicles away, as was the case when I worked for a big company.

I turned these contradictions and ambiguities into a presentation for Austin Startup Week. I was privileged to give a talk at the event, but I had been unable to market it sufficiently and therefore failed to get many attendees. Three people showed up...and one of them was a friend. I was disappointed but decided that those three were going to get the best presentation of their lives on how to deal with ambiguity in their businesses.

Here's a rundown of my points from that talk:

20 Skills, Attitudes, and Considerations an Entrepreneur Needs

1. Commit to your plan
2. Have a long-term vision
3. Create value by finding new opportunities
4. Trust what you do
5. Believe in your product/service
6. Have a can-do-anything attitude
7. Lead for everyone's success
8. See everyone as your customer
9. Make quick decisions
10. Have a winning mentality
11. Be flexible enough to learn and pivot
12. Develop a sense of urgency; move quickly to the next milestone
13. Say no to stay focused
14. Be open to listening
15. Always seek product improvement

16. Get support
17. Expect little from others
18. Understand that you are nobody's customer
19. Act with incomplete information
20. Be comfortable with "failure"

Those are twenty skills I found helpful as an entrepreneur, and I believe each one has its own identity. What happens, though, when you put the first ten of them in one column and the last ten in a second column, and then pair them against each other? Here's what you get:

1. Commitment & Flexibility
2. Long-Term & Sense of Urgency
3. New Opportunities & Staying Focused
4. Trust Yourself & Listen to Others
5. Believe Your Offering Is Good & Seek Improvement
6. Can Do Anything & Get Support
7. Lead & Expect Little
8. Everyone Is My Customer & I'm Nobody's Customer
9. Make Decisions & Incomplete Information
10. Winning Mentality & Be Comfortable with Failure

Isn't it curious how most of these are paradoxical in many ways?

You will also confront the following dynamics, which compounds what you are trying to execute:

1. Your work usually is cut out by the hardest pains and most crucial opportunities, but first you always help those around you.

2. Help is good, but you can't accept everybody's assistance, since many people will require more energy from you than what they give back to the business.

3. Money makes things go much faster, but you have a limited budget.

4. You need to act as if you are going to succeed and lay a foundation for a bright future, but you still need to go step by step and be mindful of the cash burn.

5. You may need both cold market research and burning passion.

6. You don't have time to *play* at being a leader because you will *be* a leader.

7. You need to view opportunities where others don't but operate in everyone's shared playing field.

The most perplexing situation an entrepreneur faces is when they have not succeeded or found a market. Because there is always a *yet*. Yes, it hasn't happened…*yet*.

Even when this is the case, it doesn't mean there isn't a market waiting for your product. The innate belief, of course, is that there *is* a market, even if one does not yet exist. Self-honesty becomes critical but is tempered by the element of

The most perplexing situation an entrepreneur faces is when they have not succeeded or found a market. Because there is always a yet. Yes, it hasn't happened…yet.

what's possible and the excitement that it engenders.

I concluded my talk with the suggestion that the answer to ambiguity is to have various hypotheses about your product and market and to run experiments that test them until you find the right product-market fit. Keep trying different things. Make it a numbers game until something sticks. In retrospect, though, I think that works in theory, but not always in practice. I don't believe my own earlier premise because you can run experiments all day, every day, and keep going from wrong to wrong without ever hitting the jackpot. There is a great fallacy in thinking it's all about the numbers and just trying one more time.

What's happening to you while you are trying one more time?

We all want wins. Big or small. Wins beget wins. There is a difference, though, between overcoming obstacles and having an operating company that is making and selling a product. If you spend all your energy knocking down walls, how do you ever discover the path of least resistance? You can begin to feel as if you are moving through a pitch-dark tunnel. You can crawl, going slowly, touching the wall for reference and taking the next step, but is that how you want to make progress? Is that how you want to live your life?

We all want wins. Big or small. Wins beget wins.

Trying one more thing becomes a trap. The fact that we didn't find our customer doesn't mean we would have if we'd tried just one more thing. What is the point of taking just one more step if you are not moving in the right direction?

I think people suffer from the same compulsion when seeking romance on a dating app, believing the love of their lives could be waiting for them on the next swipe. Sure, their true love *might* be just one swipe away, but there is a fallacy to the idea that we need someone to complete us as people. We get caught up in the energy of desperation, whether that is prompted by a desire to have a successful startup or find our life partner.

The journey is as important as the destination.

Sacrifice never scared me. I thought, though, that there ought to be more joy in the experience of a startup, regardless of the struggle. My efforts to get through that dark tunnel and find the light at the other end did teach me one indelible lesson.

crash course

The journey is as important as the destination. And that, as much as this idea of light at the end of the tunnel, motivates us. It's light in the middle of the tunnel—the internal and external clarity—that's going to make the crossing possible.

chapter 21

New Lottery Tickets

....

THE KEY LESSON every first-time entrepreneur learns is that creating and running a business can be profoundly challenging both intellectually and emotionally. You also learn to adapt and be flexible as situations change. I tried to maintain an inner clarity while remaining open to the right kind of external guidance. There were always times when I was looking for someone to trust who knew more than I did about various issues. Everything was about seeking answers; sometimes that meant I had to push harder, and sometimes it meant taking a detour to get where I wanted. Very often an entrepreneur needs to make sure they have the courage to come to a situation without a predefined answer, and surprisingly, this is not that easy. The best approach is to have as many tools as possible in your toolbox of experience and learning, and to know which one fits the situation you are confronting.

You also need to know that a lot of generalized advice might not work. Just because others have succeeded does not mean that their experience correlates to yours. As Naval

As entrepreneur, investor, and deep thinker Naval Ravikant explains:

> If you ask a specific person what worked for them, very often it's just like they are reading out the exact set of things that worked for them, which may not be applicable for you. They are just reading you their winning lottery ticket numbers. It's a little glib. There is something to be learned from them, but you can't just take their exact circumstance and map it onto yours. The best founders I know—they listen and read to everyone. But then they ignore everybody and they make up their own mind. They have their own internal model of how to apply things to their situation and they do not hesitate to discard information. If you survey enough people all the advice will cancel to zero. So you do have to have your own point of view and when something is sent your way, you have to very quickly decide: is that true? Is that true outside of the context of what that person applied it in? Is it true in my context? And then, do I want to apply it? You have to reject most of the advice, but you have to listen to and read enough of it to know what to reject and what to accept.[12]

Creating a winning startup is about fine-tuning functionalities and processes and growing more and more resourceful.

A sensitivity is also required to make certain you keep your business activities on point. That will be your best chance of skipping the dreadful task of going from wrong to wrong and from mistake to mistake. There will be much trial and error, but if you have learned from your experiences, you are prepared for what each moment asks of you, whether that is continuing the same course, pivoting, or taking a pause to reflect and analyze before proceeding. I believe entrepreneurs ought to be as unbiased as possible about seeing their own situations and deciding upon the smartest actions and next steps to take.

If you have learned from your experiences, you are prepared for what each moment asks of you, whether that is continuing the same course, pivoting, or taking a pause to reflect and analyze before proceeding.

One of our shortcomings as humans is that we often respond to situations with predefined learned behaviors, and they make us seem more like a mechanistic program than a conscious person. We need to analyze, first, before we react. What if every time you went on a date with someone, your urges maniacally poured out through your eyes and you had already decided—possibly in a subconscious way—that, *I need to have sex, no matter what.*

Maybe you think the opposite: *I am going to be a gentleman and not have sex, even if she wants to.* You have created a disposition before you even know the facts.

When I was living in Miami, I went on a couple of dates with a beautiful woman I thought looked a lot like the actress Jessica Alba. She was, in fact, one of the most beautiful girls I had ever gone out with. I was additionally intrigued by the fact that she was from Cali, Colombia, which is where I was living while working on the first draft of this book.

When I met her, I was living in South Beach, and she drove to my place and parked near my apartment. After our evening together, which I thought was wonderful, I assumed the time had arrived to say good-bye, and I didn't invite her up to my place, which was a fool's move. She said she wanted to come up and see the apartment, but I didn't offer the invitation because I had this silly idea that I wanted to create the impression of a guy who was patient and respectful and wanted a meaningful relationship, not just sex. I had a wrongheaded and predefined version of how things were going to work out that evening, and I was living my life with too much control and not being open to the circumstances I encountered.

You probably already figured out that I never saw her again.

We often miss what is right in front of us because of fear disguised as control. What if, instead, we played life more like an improvisation show in which we said yes to most things? Before long, we might wake up in a magical place and have no idea how we even got there. Whether that's a regular guy like me

We often miss what is right in front of us because of fear disguised as control.

kissing Jessica Alba beneath the tropical moonlight or just enjoying freedom from the tight constraints of your inhibiting mind, those are better places to be, and sometimes you can get there simply by failing.

I will concede, though, that hearing the struggles of another entrepreneur would likely not have prevented mine, since I wanted to have my own experience. However, hearing their stories may have helped me to be more prepared. It's always good to know what you are getting into if that's knowable. I had plenty of theoretical knowledge at my disposal but not the patience or personality to entertain that important information. I wanted to go ahead and "just do my thing," which I did.

I deeply value observation, curiosity, and original thinking. I enjoy finding asymmetric relationships, but above all, I love having my own experience. In the case of my company, I foolishly wasn't willing to slow down and do careful analyses. Such a tactic had the potential to improve my decision-making and could mitigate risk by a factor of as much as 90 percent, and the loss of speed would drop our likelihood of success by 1 percent.

How foolish was I to rush ahead without all the knowledge demanded by the situation?

chapter 22

Throwing Spears

....

I STILL ADMIT to an incapacity to draw solid conclusions after the fact, even as my stubbornness wears down. I can see how more awareness of markets, products, and investors would have been sensible and might have altered the outcome. I certainly wasn't uninformed and capricious, but more data and information might have written a different ending for Plushkies. I can't say that for certain, though.

However, I did learn much worth sharing.

Dr. Joe Dispenza, a scientist and lecturer who says he cured his spine, which had been injured in an accident, with only his mind, defines "*personality* as the combination of our thoughts, behaviors, and emotions."[13] Almost all of us want to change our personal realities to have more health, more love, more money, or deeper relationships. Not that many of us, though, are putting in the work to change our personalities, which is striking because our "personalities create our personal realities."[14] Every day, people have 90 percent of the same thoughts and reproduce similar emotions. And every day, people go through the exact same motions and habits of behavior. "The redundancy of that cycle becomes a subconscious program. So now they've lost their free will to a program."[15]

What's worse is that any meaningful change requires awareness of our default mode and a conscious choice to do something new, even something dramatically different. To not feel like we are always going back to square one, it's important that we pay attention to our state of being.

> *When you do something new, truly new, you can become someone else and enter a new realm. This is when unique creations may happen.*

When you do something new, truly new, you can become someone else and enter a new realm. This is when unique creations may happen.

Grit

In her TED Talk, Angela Lee Duckworth identifies grit as a significant predictor of success in many different contexts. I can't imagine an area in which "passion and perseverance for very long-term goals," as she defines grit, could be as relevant as in entrepreneurship. If this mountain of difficult experiences happened to me over many years, it's because I didn't fold after the first setback. I "stuck with my future day in, day out, not just for the week, not just for the month, but for years."[16]

Clarity

Grit and determination are absolutely crucial to success, but unfortunately, they're not always enough. We can think of them as the engine of the car. But the right direction can only be achieved through clarity: the capacity to process the available information, understand a situation, and make sensible and practical decisions.

Don't Put the Cart Before the Horse,
aka, Know Your Customer

Keep things in the right order. This one is painfully obvious. First, figure out your reason for being in business—what you are doing, why, and for whom—and then optimize and scale all you want.

We should have tried harder to pay more to get more product samples and not have rushed into full production. Focus on product market-fit with those samples. Manufacturing and setting up logistics and operations for a medium company when your customer assumptions have not been validated is not something I recommend. Unless, of course, you are like me, and you have to learn the hard lessons to make them stick.

Be Ambitious and "Don't Scale"

In a panel in Barcelona, tech founder Màrius Montmany shared how his company REVER was accepted in Y Combinator as they were trying to change the trillion-dollar "return industry" in a very rudimentary fashion. His product was an Excel spreadsheet, and he did the refunds himself using his own Revolut account.

"For sure that's not going to be the solution in the future but if you have done it like that until now there must be potential" was Y Combinators acknowledgment of how they were "making something people wanted."[17]

In the same panel, Arnau Navarro, founder of Y Combinator Haddock, added, "the focus is in pain pain pain, problem solution. Forget about scaling. Do things that don't scale and when you have a 100 customers that love you then figure out how to make the solution scalable."[18]

A loving customer is the answer you need to have a company, not something you should be figuring out three years after launch. If you can't profile your customer and identify why they might be excited to buy—or use—your product, you don't have a customer—or a company.

How Competitive Is the Marketplace?

This is something I also didn't pay attention to and didn't find out until I was trying to reach buyers. As I mentioned earlier in the book, I once heard that more new products try to enter the market in a year than the number of products currently in the market. This is astounding. I haven't confirmed this, but I wouldn't be surprised if it's true. The mere assertion that this is true means it is shocking that the landscape is so competitive. A crowded marketplace ought to be an assumption, though, because the Internet has inspired people to try things they might not have tried a few decades earlier, and not as many resources are required to create a toy, food, a more efficient electric fan, or fraud detection through AI.

The Best Tech Doesn't Always Win

Product messages must be made clear, and someone or something needs to be sharing with the CEO the efforts of raising awareness for customer acquisition and brand development.

Do Not Live in La-La Land

Just because my company was registered on the same block as Whole Foods' headquarters, and I thought my product was a great fit for their stores, I shouldn't have assumed they would be interested in offering any help. Or that they would have even given me the time of day. The lesson is that there has to be depth and grounding in your offerings, something that others find valuable.

Sometimes being cute is enough, but more often, it's not.

Be Realistically Optimistic

You need to have an awareness that during some part of the entrepreneurial movie, an "enemy" will likely show up. You don't need to prepare in advance for every potential kind of adversary that would freeze you, and you don't need to plant a seed in your consciousness that all that can will go wrong, will end up cattywampus. You should not, however, be caught off guard when something does go sideways and fails. Being more prepared than I was for this will likely help you identify what's happening so you can make smarter decisions.

Be Resourceful

This one I expected, but not to the degree that it was needed. I felt constantly stretched when it came to resources needed to do the job. Sometimes, the issue was the budget, and other times, I ran out of mental capacity and energy. Each of those was critical to creating a product, growing the business, and solving problems.

Prioritize

Define key milestones. Identify three goals per quarter and align monthly and weekly initiatives to their achievement. Even one meaningful daily goal will give you a sense of accomplishment at the end of each day. Too much "fog"—in the form of distractions and meaningless tasks or "busywork"— can cause you to lose sight of your goals and, eventually, lose control of the company and even your own life. If you find yourself deviating from your plan several days in a row, either you need to be more disciplined or you need to reprioritize things. Reprioritization should be detailed and your commitment unwavering.

Habits versus Outcomes

Focus on what you can control. During my time as an entrepreneur, I tried to distinguish between positive outcomes and the habits that led me to those accomplishments. And in my brief moments of glorious clarity, I tried to focus on what I could control—being disciplined and doing what I said I was going to do. Those weren't goals I just shared with another person in a conversation. I wrote them down, scheduled when they needed to get done, and made a plan to complete the work.

Give Your Best (and Be Intentional about It)

I know this is another bit of advice that seems obvious, but *giving your best* doesn't necessarily mean trying harder. Sometimes it may mean slowing down, which involves taking a long, slow breath. Look at your situation from a different perspective. Maybe even run in the opposite direction, if that makes sense.

I've seen many sports coaches share strategies to turn things around after a losing streak. Some are good. Some . . . are not. The one I've heard the most is this:

> Giving your best *doesn't necessarily mean trying harder. Sometimes it may mean slowing down, which involves taking a long, slow breath. Look at your situation from a different perspective. Maybe even run in the opposite direction, if that makes sense.*

"There are three things we need to do: work harder, work harder, and work harder." When I hear this, my stomach twists and turns. If all you do is more of the same thing, but you just do it harder, you may simply fail harder.

Before going faster and stronger, make sure you are heading in the right direction. Choose to think differently. Be smarter. Be kinder. Give more. It's always important to have an open mind, which enables you to act from a deeper level of knowledge of what each moment requires without always pulling from the same bag of tricks. Give 100 percent but be clear about what that involves and how you define it. Better to use skill than strength.

Choose the Path of Least Resistance
You have a lot on your plate. If you have a chance to make the path smoother and friendlier and skip the hard work that has a low ROI, make that move. For instance, I was once asked by an angel investor to send him a business plan, and I didn't think that was the best use of my time. I provided a two-pager and asked him to meet in person for a full presentation. He agreed, but nothing ever came of it.

Success
What is your definition of success? Is it borrowed from society, or have you thought it through with great care to give it a shape that makes you happy? Is it static or dynamic? Is it supporting you and making your life kinder and fuller? Or is it a heavy

burden? Can you be loving or at least kind to yourself if you don't achieve success in that form?

Make Requests

Entrepreneurs make requests, proposals, suggestions—whatever is needed to move our plans forward. At the beginning, we are always playing offense. I think Tim Ferriss puts it nicely:

> To become "successful," you have to say "yes" to a lot of experiments. To learn what you're best at, or what you're most passionate about, you have to throw a lot against the wall. Once your life shifts from pitching outbound to defending against inbound, however, you have to ruthlessly say "no" as your default. Instead of throwing spears, you're holding the shield.[19]

We are not at the shift yet (or perhaps we are not Tim Ferriss yet), so for now we are the ones constantly throwing spears. Nobody knows what we do, and nobody understands the potential of what we do as we believe it to be, so we need to be convincing, persuading, achieving, articulating, demonstrating, charming . . . you get it.

Remember Fun?

Do one thing a day just for fun. When you're blindly driven by heart and hustle it's easy to forget about yourself. Do

Do one thing a day just for fun. When you're blindly driven by heart and hustle it's easy to forget about yourself.

Do something every day that makes you feel good, that brings you joy, and reclaims your individuality.

things for you, not only for your company. You are more than a means for your company's success. Do something every day that makes you feel good, that brings you joy, and reclaims your individuality. If there is no fun involved in what you are doing, there isn't much point in proceeding.

Know Yourself

What are you really trying to do? Is making the world a better place a realistic goal? What motivates you? Why are you really doing this? Deep inside, are you an artist, a builder, a seller, an experimenter, an achiever, or are you someone trying to escape from something? As much as I was surprised by how little I sold, I was positively surprised by my capacity to create products. I am not a big fan of marketing, though. Not because I don't think it's valuable, but because it might be the difference between success and failure, and it doesn't come naturally to me. I have no idea of how to sell, and methodical market research is certainly not my cup of tea.

Know Your Biases

An important part of knowing yourself is knowing your biases. The naïve and inexperienced me used to think that all ideas would succeed. Many years ago, three high school friends of mine opened a bar in our hometown of Zaragoza, Spain. It bothered me that I couldn't join the opportunity because I was living abroad and thought they were going to do great. It turned out to be a train wreck.

Only now after seeing lots of ideas not working after originally thinking they would, I'm starting to question my initial impressions. On the opposite side, I have a cousin who has analysis paralysis and is incapable of taking a risk. The idea is to learn from our experiences and biases and develop a more sophisticated judgment.

What's in It for Me?

I offer this question not from the point of view we are used to of some kind of financial reward, but from the point of view of what is in this situation for me? What is the learning, or the gift I need to unveil? What can I see about myself in how this other person is behaving?

Self-Actualize

Use rejection to evolve. Failure will always inform success. Adam Grant, an organizational psychologist at the Wharton School and *New York Times* bestselling author, points out, "Every resume and bio that you put together is basically just stringing one success or accomplishment next to another, and we kind of erase all the failures in between. We should all be more open about the challenges we have faced."[20]

Make every attempt to turn into the person or company that wouldn't be rejected in the same circumstances in the future. And give yourself as many opportunities as you can.

Failures and how we deal with them provide a more complete picture of who we are as a person and an entrepreneur. Who goes through life without failing? It's easy not to fail if you don't try anything.

I tried. And I tried. And I tried. And that, eventually, changed my future.

chapter 23

Driven by Self-Expression

....

WHEN A PERSON is inclined toward entrepreneurialism, they eventually reach a moment where they have an idea and must decide whether to pursue its potential. Seth Godin, the always-original and wise author of many marketing books, recommends sharing the idea with ten friends and seeing if it spreads. I think that's great advice. Unfortunately, my personality lacked patience for such a tactic. I have always tended to act more on impulse. Even a simple commonsense test like that seemed too methodical for me.

My interest wasn't in checking whether I *should* do it; my interest was in *doing* it.

Was that a mistake? Consider my own experience with the iPhone. As I mentioned earlier, when the first iPhone came out, I thought it wasn't for me. Now, though, I get a new one every couple of years.

In his book *Crossing the Chasm*,[21] author Geoffrey A. Moore explains that there are different kinds of customers

> *I don't like cutting ideas down at their roots. I want to plant them and give them air to breathe and sunlight to grow.*

with different speeds of adoption, from innovators to laggards. Selecting the wrong customer sample to validate my idea could have killed it before giving it any real chance. Even my inability to articulate properly, or to pitch a premature idea, might have been fatal. Some companies managed a big success after pivoting from their original idea. Some people err on the side of needing too much reassurance to take a step forward, whereas I tend to default in the other direction and just start walking in the direction I have chosen. I don't like cutting ideas down at their roots. I want to plant them and give them air to breathe and sunlight to grow.

With this convenient insight in my back pocket, no market research was going to stop me from giving in to my impulses and chasing what my heart said was a good idea. Nothing was going to deter me. Even one thousand potential customers telling me no was not an impediment. I don't think I was interested in listening. What am I suggesting to you? I hope it's obvious—that you study both your motives and your biases.

I wanted to make an impact and change the world—while also making a lot of money—but there was something deeper. I can't name it, exactly, but imagine that someone told you, "The person you're interested in doesn't like you, and everybody knows it."

I'm the kind of person whose response would be, "OK, I'm going to ask her out and hear it for myself." Who knows? Maybe Steve Jobs did ask ten of his friends before launching the iPhone, and I just didn't happen to be one of them.

Society doesn't know whether or not it will like vacuum cleaners that operate without bags, so go ahead and express your genius by making one. The more "out there" and edgy you become, the less likely your potential customers may know what they want. It's just as likely that a test customer may tell you they like the taste of one drink more than another, but then they don't buy it. How could that be? Because a "taste" isn't necessarily representative of the customer's entire experience with your product.

A "taste" isn't necessarily representative of the customer's entire experience with your product.

Since the invention of cola, the rivalry between Pepsi and Coca-Cola (i.e., Coke) has existed. The data shows that most people prefer Coke products to Pepsi products. However, in a blind taste test, Diet Pepsi was preferred over Diet Coke. This has been coined the "Pepsi Paradox."[22]

In another battle of the "cola wars," in 1983 Coca-Cola created New Coke, a sweeter cola that outperformed both Pepsi and the classic formulation of Coke in blind taste tests. But people don't drink a half ounce of soda in real life; they drink whole cans, and they thought New Coke tasted way too sweet. Thus, Coca-Cola went back to its original formula.[23]

Not only does the entrepreneur have the complex task of uncovering the real needs of their customers, but they also need to be prepared to answer questions — especially from investors. When pitching to potential investors, entrepreneurs will benefit from clarifying early the "pain point" their company or product is easing and what the specific problem is that they would fix. The other critical bit of information is getting reliable data about market size. Again, this is not as easy as it sounds. What would have been the estimated market size for Uber? The total market for yellow-and-black cabs? Or for Airbnb? Very short-term rentals in other people's houses? The problem with these estimates is that we estimate from what we know, and that is limited to . . . well . . . only what we know.

We estimate from what we know, and that is limited to... well...only what we know.

Driven by Self-Expression

Entrepreneurs are also often advised to "find a problem, solve it for one person (ideally for themselves), and then solve it for many people." Plushkies did not do this. We did the opposite and began with something I thought was creative and then looked for a market. We were a solution looking for a problem. My high-speed brain turned into a hammer that saw nails everywhere. I sometimes wonder about Google in terms of solving a problem. Did founders Larry Page and Sergey Brin intuitively know the importance of *search* in the future of the Internet? Or did they solve a technical and business problem in an innovative way and thus were able to find millions of users? I'd lean toward the latter.

Children are often asked a question that I think needs to be dramatically revised. They are often asked, "What do you want to be when you grow up?" I think it's more important that we inquire of bright young minds, "What problems do you hope to someday solve?" If we may split hairs for a second, though, in the case of Plushkies, I don't know that I was trying to find a problem to solve as much as I was attempting to discover a channel—commercial as much as emotional—in which I could express myself.

These are intrinsic questions every entrepreneur must ask themselves before making the leap into business. Be honest with yourself. Are you doing this for yourself or for others? Do you have an urge to express your creativity, make an impact, or make money? Do you want to have a project just so you can stay busy? Do you want to master

Be honest with yourself. Are you doing this for yourself or for others? Do you have an urge to express your creativity, make an impact, or make money? Do you want to have a project just so you can stay busy? Do you want to master the art of entrepreneurship? Do you like the idea of being a CEO? What is the number one driver of your decision to start a business?

the art of entrepreneurship? Do you like the idea of being a CEO? What is the number one driver of your decision to start a business?

In my case, it was *self-expression.*

My attitude of listening to the market only after I had something to sell could be considered arrogant, perhaps even suicidal, if the main goal had been to make money.

I can see an entire set of conflicting dynamics surrounding success in the band Green Day's story. After achieving big success with their album *Dookie*, the California band discovered that it can sometimes be as much of a shock to receive more than one expects as it can be to receive less:

Driven by Self-Expression

One day in 1995, on Haight Ashbury in San Francisco, Billie Joe Armstrong was accosted by a stranger, someone who "looked like a really early '80s English postcard punk." The character walked with the swagger of an angry young man, and upon seeing the Green Day frontman before him, issued from his mouth a volley of insults. In short, Billie Joe was told that he was a "sellout."[24]

A part of me used to romanticize failure as a sign of being true to oneself. This is counterproductive because it makes failure the only outcome of authenticity. It assumes the only two options in life are either being a failure or a sellout. I'm glad to have matured and to no longer have that perception. I do feel you can have your cake and eat it too, but first you must bake the damn cake.

Putting your heart and drive into the task but leaving your common sense out to mitigate risks is like driving a car with wheels and a big engine but no steering wheel. That is how I often felt: a big dream, a big vision, and a lack of direction to get to sales.

And yes, of course I wanted to achieve my big vision of having a toy for each country in the world, and a movie, and a theme park, and the big bucks, and even the vague goal of "making the world a better place." The more honest and committed we are with our work, while focused on something we

The more honest and committed we are with our work, while focused on something we love, the more likely we will be to succeed.

Understand better what people want, and assume less, specifically about how you are going to reach your audience. And learn. Always be learning.

love, the more likely we will be to succeed. Remember, too, the best effort, in my view, involves doing some market research, understanding product market fit, and being methodical. My preference was to avoid the intense market data dive, and I think I paid for that. There were other causes that contributed to Plushkies failing, but poor market research might have been central to our flop.

I hope you do care about those things, especially if you want to make some money. Understand better what people want, and assume less, specifically about how you are going to reach your audience. And learn. Always be learning. I feel like I learned a lot, and I also feel like a big part of what I learned would have been good to know before I put all my savings—and even money I didn't have—into my venture. The lesson was learned. Did I mention I learned a lot?

And it will guide what comes next.

chapter 24

A Crash Course in Entrepreneurial Sanity

AFTER EVERYTHING you've learned about my experience, this is probably a good time to reiterate that this is a book about the entrepreneur, not the enterprise. I don't know how to build a big company, but I do know what an entrepreneur goes through in the attempt.

Entrepreneurs are not machines that manufacture companies in an assembly line. By nature, the job of the entrepreneur is to create a company out of their ideas and to build something that is new and unique. Nobody hands us a job with the title of *founder*. You can't even interview for it. If you are the first founder, you can only get the title by giving it to yourself.

> *By nature, the job of the entrepreneur is to create a company out of their ideas and to build something that is new and unique.*

Being an all-in entrepreneur is an intense way of living that generates emotional responses to various circumstances and unexpected outcomes.

Doing something new is usually not easy, and it comes with challenges that tend to provoke emotions. Being an all-in entrepreneur is an intense way of living that generates emotional responses to various circumstances and unexpected outcomes. But most entrepreneurs don't talk about such things when they are grinding away toward success.

I imagine most high-power lawyers, pilots, architects, teachers, and other professionals don't portray their emotions publicly either. Our culture doesn't accept such honesty most of the time. In fact, it's probably only in sports that we see athletes share their joy after winning a competition, or breaking a racket in frustration after a bad shot. Even in many artistic disciplines, we see the artist's emotions expressed through their art rather than through their physical self.

I noticed this lack of emotional expression throughout my time working on Plushkies, and I always gave it thought. Why are we not more open about our feelings, including our feelings about how we are doing in business and our professional endeavors? I think the reasons are obvious:

- People are disconnected and have learned to function outwardly while neglecting their inward emotions.

- Emotional openness requires sensitivity, willingness, and time to "feel our feelings."

- Our emotions are often unpleasant, which can make them seem bad or inconvenient.

- We fear that honest emotional expression might cause damage to our image and reputation, changing how other people see us.

- We avoid putting others in situations we might judge as uncomfortable, as most people will likely not be adept at dealing with them.

We may have an idea of how we *should* feel that does not match reality—how we actually, sincerely feel. It's good to think positively, but it's just as important to be honest with yourself.

Imagine you've put a lot of effort and hope into a presentation for an investor, and that investor says he is not interested. That hurts. Yes, you can brush it off, tell yourself, *It's OK, there are more investors out there,* and keep going with your life, but that's just accommodating it in your head. Your heart says, *It hurts,* while your head says, *It's OK,* and that creates a disconnection. Emotions do not exist to be overcome; they must be recognized, connected with, and allowed. In my case,

Emotions do not exist to be overcome; they must be recognized, connected with, and allowed.

as you've probably noticed, I simply did not channel in a healthy way my emotional responses to various situations regarding Plushkies.

Or maybe I did.

Honestly, I'm not even sure.

Perhaps I managed and properly processed my emotions a thousand times and then they reappeared. Even in hindsight, it's hard to know. If I felt stuck a hundred times, it must also be true that I got *unstuck* a hundred times. I did, at least, proceed, even though I was not successful. But I am not talking here about success. With Plushkies, I did not display any great entrepreneurial talents. I still don't have any final answers to the questions I kept proposing. Each situation is different, each story is different, each

Each situation is different, each story is different, each moment is different, and each of us is different.

moment is different, and each of us is different.

This is a book about recognizing the founder as an individual who is not only doing something new but is also doing something meaningful for themselves and often for the wider world. And that entrepreneur has a lot at stake with loans, mortgages, other people's money, jobs that support families, and their own and their employees' personal dreams. I can't write a recipe for a better cocktail to stir up emotional responses. I think self-honesty is essential and success is not possible without allowing yourself to regularly pause for a few minutes to connect with what you feel. Stop worrying for a second about what's happening with your company and take a couple of deep breaths. Then come back to yourself.

I tried to understand these things and follow my own advice, but my default state was tired and wired. That's how I've spent a big part of my life, even before being an entrepreneur.

I was frequently without much energy and vitality but still pumping out thoughts, spinning them in all directions. Why couldn't I rest? Because I was hyperactive, overstimulated, and did not trust myself or others enough to relax.

I advise all entrepreneurs to attend to themselves. As Dr. Joe Dispenza says, "You can take all your nutrients, work out, do pilates, do yoga, do your breathing, do all of that, get your body chemically balanced, physically balanced, but if you are not going to get your body emotionally balanced. . . forget it. Because the moment you get emotional your body literally goes to the past. That's the one that matters the most."[25]

Paying attention to this aspect of your well-being as an entrepreneur is not a small thing, particularly when things don't go as anticipated and roadblocks begin to appear. Your company may not grow as you want it to, but that doesn't mean you should feel alone, rejected, and unattended—both by the world and by yourself.

I learned a great deal and developed a broad range of ideas as a startup businessman. Managing emotional health was just one facet of my education. Others came from observation, talking to others, reading books, and listening to podcasts. The insights I am sharing come from my own experience along with a spiritual journey that took me on a six-month meditation retreat to Uruguay with the Isha Judd Educating for Peace Foundation after I finally decided to let go of my entrepreneurial dreams.

I am still unable to make a full account of all I learned during that process, which also involved one hundred fifty other students who became my extended family. Much of my initial long-term spiritual guidance came from Isha Judd's book *Why Walk When You Can Fly?* The system she describes for spiritual fulfillment is accessible to any individual. I also learned from my friend Rajani Santosh, a tantra teacher who was a fellow participant in the six-month retreat. Rajani wrote the book *Tantra Ahora*, which has not just helped me to heal after my Plushkies experience but has helped me to understand who I am and how I want to live my life.

Consider what follows as a crash course in entrepreneurial sanity survival.

A Crash Course in Entrepreneurial Sanity

Breathe

Start with an easy one. Slow down. Take three deep breaths. Let all of your thoughts go, and try to touch the beauty of the specific moment in time in which you are living.

Pause

I attended several Digital Detoxes with the Camp Grounded group,[13] which is a kind of summer camp for adults. At the camp, participants are not allowed to talk about work or use their real names, and they have to surrender all their technology when they enter. The first step we took was to give ourselves a nickname, and then we were given what was called a "pause" bracelet, which helped us learn how to pause and anchor ourselves. Try that right where you're at—be present in doing nothing.

Meditate

Hundreds of books have been written about meditation but for me, in its simplest form it is befriending yourself exactly as you are in this moment. Dropping all ideas and beliefs, slowing down, and coming into your own unknown present experience. Learning to observe your mind and body's internal movements without reacting to them. Staying with your deepest experience (calm, agitations, emotions, and physical sensations) with honesty and without judgment regardless of how uncomfortable it is. Trusting your heart.

Self-Honesty

I can't overstate how important it is to be honest with yourself about how you feel. Don't *wallow* in your emotions; *connect* with them. Denial is not healthy. There's absolutely nothing wrong with how you feel. If that's what you feel, then that's what you feel. The only thing that can make that wrong is your mind. Practice choosing when you want to listen to what your emotions are telling you and when you don't. Your brain is smarter than you think, and it is running a very tricky program. The problem with the program is that it doesn't care about your well-being; its interest is in your survival.

Be honest with yourself about how you feel. Don't wallow in your emotions; connect with them.

Sadness, anger, and desperation are normal, organic bodily functions as essential as passing waste from your digestive system. The question is, *What are you going to do with those emotions?*

Find a healthy way to connect to and express your emotions. Here's an analogy that is just crass enough to help you remember it: You don't hold your poop for weeks at a time, but you also don't relieve yourself in your neighbor's front yard for the sake of convenience either. The same goes for your emotions. Don't hold them in, but also be wise about where, when, and how you fully express them.

The alternative is carrying the turmoil within you that could be detonated at any chance, which certainly won't make you very productive or relaxed. You can choose to be aware of how you feel and find a healthy way to release it, or you can allow emotional angst to govern you and make your business decisions for you.

This can turn you into a marionette that is stuck and frustrated without knowing the cause. You can potentially become overwhelmed, confused, hopeless, and, yes, even clueless. It's even possible to be clueless about why you are clueless because you have an emotional buildup that keeps creating pressure. Find a safe place or the right support and connect with caring and perspective. Let it all go. Empty twenty pounds from your backpack. Understand what is going on and how you got there.

I frequently don't feel my emotions, but if I'm trying to work and feel stuck, unfocused, and unproductive for too long, it is safe for me to assume there's an unidentified and unresolved emotional cause beneath the surface that needs my attention.

Four Basic Emotions

I am neither a psychiatrist nor any type of medical expert, but I've learned much from my entrepreneurial sufferings and commitment to personal growth. My insights come from those experiences. I know that if your body is full of anger and sadness, it's going to be very difficult for your mind to calm down and be productive. In the Isha System, we work with four basic emotions. The better you understand these emotions, the better you can deal with your emotional health.

1. **Joy:** Expressed through a smile, laugh, pleasure

2. **Sadness:** Comes often with tears

3. **Anger:** Can be released by hitting or screaming

4. **Fear:** Less universal since it's expressed differently by people and their circumstances. Crying, hitting a punching bag, and even screaming can help open a path for fear to dissipate.

Pataleta

I like this Spanish word that describes a child's temper tantrum while lying in bed and facing upward. Have yourself a *pataleta* and see how you feel afterward. This process can help you to release physical and mental tension, and who doesn't want to be a kid again? Plus, you've got to admit that *pataleta* is a much more fun term than *temper tantrum*.

Preventive

Consider doing a preventive. Shake up your body in the morning with a *pataleta* to move the energy and allow underlying emotions to bubble up. Beat up a pillow or a yoga mat to

256

subdue and release your emotions. Even if you don't feel like doing it, give it a go and see if it doesn't clear your head and get your creative juices flowing.

It's Just Stress

Emotions regarding your business can turn into stress. But not all emotions are bad. They are just messages waiting to be heard, and you need to listen. Stress can disappear when it's allowed to flow through you, and that is possible through self-awareness. No one wants to live under stress—unless you wear your inner turmoil as a badge of honor or a measure of your importance. Some people equate stress with success and are therefore unwilling to release it, but I don't recommend this.

Not all emotions are bad. They are just messages waiting to be heard, and you need to listen. Stress can disappear when it's allowed to flow through you, and that is possible through self-awareness.

Feel, Move, Let Go

After shaking, moving, hitting, and having a *pataleta*, you need to sit down, catch your breath, relax, and ask yourself what's happening in your body. This is very different from asking yourself how you want to feel or should feel. The answer is not in your head; it's in your body. Connect curiosity and innocence with your emotions and physical sensations. Notice what's really happening in your physical and emotional body. This is the heart of meditation—simply *being with what is*. Once you have awareness of what is happening, you can allow it to move and to be.

Try to express the emotions described above and nudge them into moving through you but without forcing the issue. It may be possible to let them wash over you or go through you with no impediment, or they may want to hang around for some time. In that case, gently stay present with them.

American neuroscientist Andrew Huberman states:

The more often that you can ask yourself what am I really feeling right now? How do I feel? And this is so critical, the more that you force yourself not to use broad labels, and understand that good, ok, and bad are not emotions. . . . Putting more nuance and specificity on your emotions but also touching into your own emotional state more times per day clearly has positive impacts for mood and mental health.[27]

We are not trying to force ourselves into a particular state of being, but to be with whatever we are feeling, regardless of whether it's pleasant or not. We are trying to be loving with ourselves, not violently suppressing, denying, or forcing our feelings.

Telling yourself a false positive affirmation, such as "everything is fine" when it's not, can produce a disconnect between the message you are telling yourself in your mind and the agitation in your body. At the same time, wallowing in your emotions with self-pity or drama is not productive either since that is only going to generate more emotions and blockages.

We are honestly connecting with our inner self, digging through the subtle layers of our human experience. Simply put, we're asking, *What is happening within me right now?* And we are listening to the response with our body to connect with the power of the charge, dissipate it, and bounce back.

Come Home to Peace

After the emotions have done whatever they need to do and you are feeling calmer, it becomes possible to enjoy your peace and congratulate yourself for taking responsibility for how you feel. If your emotions don't diminish, you can still stay connected to them by "accompanying yourself." As this happens, you'll be ready to consider new alternatives and behaviors. Openness, acceptance, and humility will bring calmness and flexibility. But don't try telling your body how you want it to feel. Be receptive and listen to what it has to tell you. You may not like what it has to say but listen anyway.

Total Responsibility: From Victim to Creator

When you begin to see yourself as a victim, consider if there is anything you did that got you into that situation. Is it possible you created the situation yourself? Is there a pattern you are repeating? Was there a red flag you missed? Could you have been more prepared? Or content? Could you have been more responsible? What is the little game you are playing that doesn't serve you anymore?

Despite all the challenges I encountered with my startup, I could still see how I had put myself in that position, how I had driven myself into that corner. This allowed me to see that what I did mattered, especially my choices, and that I was not a complete victim of mean or angry outside forces.

You are the creator of your circumstances.

If you had chosen something different, you'd be in a different position. Maybe happier, possibly sadder. Maybe more successful, possibly a failure. No matter what, you must start looking at your actions and their consequences with the same intensity with which you may be blaming the outside world. This enables you to start seeing for yourself that you are not a victim. Rather, you are the creator of your circumstances.

Alternatively, you can stick to doing what you are doing. You know, all the things that create the results you don't want—and then blame it on your partner, the market, a politician, or an investor.

I was guilty of that. I just kept on doing more and more of what, deep down, I knew wasn't working. And my misperception spilled over onto other people as well. I expected people to act a certain way because I thought that's how *I* would have acted—or at least how I wanted *them* to act. But that wasn't fair to either of us. Those stress-induced blinders only lead to even more limited vision and greater frustration.

Watch Your Thoughts

Learn to watch your thoughts and see them as birds singing. One of my favorite teachers at my six-month retreat told me, "If my mind tells me I'm useless or unworthy, I don't listen to it. If it tells me I'm great, I don't listen to that, either. What does it know about me? It's just a program." And it's true—the fact that your thoughts come from your brain doesn't make them any truer.

Exercise

Work out, move, take care of yourself. Be in nature. Do things that fulfill you. Participate in whatever will recognize and celebrate you. You are not just a means to build a company. You are a deserving human being, whether you closed a big deal or raised capital or not.

Speak Your Truth

Surely you will meet people with more money and power than you, but develop the muscle of speaking your truth.

Validate yourself and grow your own voice and confidence bigger, not smaller.

Choose Gratefulness

Be grateful and observe your focus. Are you focused on the things that go wrong or on those that go right? Some will go well, and many will simply sputter or flop. But remember that it's totally up to you to choose where your attention goes. The world may not operate how you want it to, but you can make your mind function exactly as you desire. Practice again and again bringing your attention where it best serves you.

Trust that you are creating the experience you need for your own growth. Believe the world is friendly and wants nothing bad for you, because that is almost always the case. If reading this makes you angry, move that emotion. What a great time to start your practice of connecting with what you are deeply feeling. Hit the pillow, scream at the pillow, throw it against the wall.

You may be thinking, *I have all these things to do—a product to launch, potential client meetings, funding to get—and you are telling me I also have to take care of myself? Punch pillows and have pataletas?*

There are no rules here. You don't *have* to do anything. You may take whatever course of action you want regarding your state of mind, but if you are feeling stuck and overwhelmed, and if you don't want to carry that gray cloud with you into your next meeting, you are going to have to do something about it. Consider punching a pillow until all that energy has left your system, or you might be at risk of truly having to restrain yourself during an interaction with the next innocent person who comes into your life.

What would my investor think if he knew I was crying in the mornings and beating up a pillow, I hear you asking. Who are you doing this for? And how would they even know? Besides, as with many issues today, they probably wouldn't understand. What makes outsiders experts on our lives? Whose life are you living? Yours or theirs?

You probably have this pretty picture of how things need to look. If all goes according to plan, you see a 20x exit in five years. It's like planning the perfect family with a happy marriage, two kids, a dog, and a beautiful home. But it doesn't always work like that—at least not for me and not for many of us—which is what prompted me to write this book.

When things don't go your way, maybe you need to let go of an old idea. It might increase your appreciation for other concepts and even add to your level of trust. You could suddenly think bigger, or even smaller. If there's an intimate and profound teaching in a situation, don't miss out on it because you are acting like a spoiled brat.

Moving your emotions and learning to mitigate their power over you allow you to move from victim to creator. When you feel free to cry and experience sadness, you can renew your self-image and confidence and feel stronger. There's not much as comforting as a sense of freshness about your endeavors, along with feelings of serenity, joy, and trust. There is nothing so curative for an overwhelmed entrepreneur as a good cry. You make yourself responsible for your well-being, so let go of internal pressure and, with that liberation, relocate to a new reality. From that place of clarity, it's easier to move forward with new solutions and confident decisions.

The world around us is just a stage on which we perform, isn't it? Our goal ought to be to use that idea to bring us back to ourselves, to enjoy our time here on Earth, making contributions and growing as humans. I know that might sound a bit New Agey, but it's true. Do we need things, regardless of how important they are—even our precious startup—to go a certain way for us to be happy?

I'm no longer sure how much that matters, at least beyond the idea of financial security. What does it mean that I often felt giving my best was not enough? I wanted results. I frequently feel like growth is great, but that's not what I want. In any area of my life, whether it is work, health, sports, or relationships, what I want is for things to go my way. And I had to accept that this was not always possible, and that it was dangerous to connect my happiness to those unrealistic aspirations.

I came to understand that our best is more than enough. Being kind to ourselves is essential, and far more important, than other people offering their kindness to us. How others treat you will become secondary. We need to surrender to who we are and what we feel to become our best selves. Having a whining, spoiled brat inside my head, running through my life and complaining about my lack of progress, created an internal conflict and energy drain. I was arguing with reality— boxing with God—and who can't predict the winner of that contest?

Remember the differences. Your company is not you. When you forget the distinction, misery is inevitable, and failure is just as likely.

SECTION 7

Finding the Rewards among the Risks

chapter 25

Like Ice Cream

....

I EXPECTED MANY good things to occur for me with Plushkies: sales, success, big visions of happy kids opening a window to the world and connecting with one another.

Little of that happened.

Instead, we got buyers not paying us, service providers leaving us hanging, harsh criticism, and a lack of reasonable consideration for our work.

Maybe I should have, but I frankly did not expect all the bad stuff that rose up against me.

I also admit I never anticipated, perhaps due to a lack of thorough planning, being pushed around by a drunken, bold bully. Who knew there were such adventures in becoming a founder?

There were many other developments I did not antici-pate, but these were all welcome blessings.

Despite spending most of my time rowing against the current in a precarious boat using a cheap, plastic paddle, there were many experiences from my entrepreneurial journey

Despite spending most of my time rowing against the current in a precarious boat using a cheap, plastic paddle, there were many experiences from my entrepreneurial journey that I will always cherish.

that I will always cherish. These were, even at the time, magical moments for me, found within the situations I put myself into as I did what entrepreneurs do. If I hadn't been running a startup, I wouldn't have found myself in the middle of those scenarios facing new circumstances. The goodness I found in those instances was as much of a surprise to me as the difficulties.

I made a list of some of the incredibly rewarding outcomes I did not foresee.

Early Wins

As soon as we started marketing in Austin, two families that had purchased Plushkies told me, "My son could only take two toys to his summer camp, and Fabio [our Italian toy] was one of them," and, "Our son has been sleeping with Pepe [our Mexican toy] for six months." A school in Austin had their students take a Plushky home for the weekend and then document what happened in a classroom journal, with pictures and written descriptions of all the adventures the toy had gone on with the family. The care given to and creativity expressed in those journals were phenomenal. I had never felt as rewarded with my work.

Austin Startup Community

I felt like I really got immersed in the Austin startup community. I went to countless meetups and worked the coffee shops and Mexican restaurants in one of the world's most exciting contemporary cities. I was all over town, constantly learning from others and introducing myself and my company. I made permanent friends and established lasting professional relationships.

I was happy to meet Rick Timmins, chairman of the Central Texas Angel Network, as I was launching Plushkies, which led to interactions with successful local investors who inspired me. I also was exposed to a large cohort of aspiring entrepreneurs like myself. My abiding memory of that group of entrepreneurs is that they were all passionate about their ideas, and money seemed to be only a by-product. I don't think anyone's central motivation for their startup was generating massive wealth or living the easy life.

One of those entrepreneurs exemplifies, for me, the character and determination needed to achieve success. Jesse Vickey created a company called Dinner Elf, which provides a service to prepare affordable dinners in their customers' home kitchens. His service, which costs less than takeout, shops for your groceries, cooks dinner at your home, and then cleans up after meal preparation. When we met, Jesse's company was not getting traction, which I did not find surprising. I thought what he and his wife, Nicole, were trying to pull off was extraordinarily complicated. Their proposition required expertise in food, regulations, logistics, and creating a market for a new concept.

I'll never forget one time when we met at Panera in the Arboretum, where Jesse gave me a master class in portion sizes and food transportation. I thought the detailed level at which he was problem-solving was nuts. I also didn't imagine there would be much demand for the service and thought it would be hard to find reliable "elves" who would commit to the company long-term. It wasn't that I didn't think it could work; I just considered it a very messy business. Dealing with food, strict regulations, and strangers cooking in your kitchen seemed like a hard service to scale.

Jesse explained that he built companies to solve problems he personally confronted. After graduating from college, he created a business to teach young graduates the skills and wisdom they needed in that period of their lives. When he got married and had two kids, Jesse felt he didn't really have the time or energy to do grocery shopping and meal prepping. He also didn't want to be dining out all the time, which were the circumstances that brought about the genesis of Dinner Elf. He was solving a problem that he personally had and that he assumed many working families also struggled with. Last time

I checked, his business was thriving.

Gold Badge

As mentioned earlier, I was selected to serve on a SXSW panel presentation titled "Austin As a Global Entrepreneur Landing Pad." It felt really good to be on the stage with other global entrepreneurs in the city and have my few minutes of glory in the "big leagues."

Being a Barracuda

I became good friends with Gayle Reaume, Austin's 2019 "Mentor of the Year" and CEO of Moolah U, a program that teaches kids financial literacy and leadership skills. She appointed me as their "Barracuda in Residence," which was a bit like being one of the startup judges/investors on *Shark Tank*. I had great fun watching kids think in business terms and learn financial concepts that I had known little to nothing about until I was twenty years older than they were. I also mentored several of the kids. Being of service to bright children, while sharing my experiences in life and business, was extremely rewarding.

Giving Workshops

The workshops I gave in several Austin schools were also inspiring for me and, I hope, for the children. I wore a propeller hat to take the kids on imaginary adventures all over the world. Even though their attention spans were short, I felt they were always engaged with the stories we told, toys we shared, and games we played. They seemed to love getting on board the imaginary Plushky Plane to travel the globe with me. The excitement and laughs in those workshops became the inspiration for our Plushkies books.

Children's Hospital

As part of our Kickstarter campaign, we committed to donating toys and books to a local children's hospital. We organized a visit where I intended to do a workshop to take the kids on a Plushkies global tour. I soon realized, though, that their energy was not the same as the healthy schoolchildren. I quickly adapted my plans to deliver a much more mellow and sensitive presentation. Being sensitive to their predicament, giving them a distraction, and encouraging their interest in the world was a special experience as much for me as it appeared to be for those young patients. We gave each child a Plushky toy, which I was later told many of them used as a security blanket.

My Blind Neighbor

Dogsitting for the best pup in the world, Fluffy, had many benefits, including getting to meet and socialize with my neighbors. That's how I met Brenton, who is blind. When we'd gotten to know each other a bit, I asked him about how he'd lost his sight and what he was doing in his life. He had been the victim of an unfortunate accident and yet remained full of positive energy. He shared several inspiring stories about how he managed to live independently. What I found most amazing was the fact that he was a sculptor. When he asked about me and I told him what we did at Plushkies, he was very excited. As I related more about our project, he started sharing some great ideas.

I had a couple of conversations with Brenton that were particularly moving. He thought it was going to be "so cool for blind people to understand how countries look [by feeling] their shapes." Those of us who are sighted can't even recognize challenges like this. Brenton mentioned he had recently explained to one of his blind friends how Africa appears "like an ice cream cone you are trying to grab." Thrilled by his interest, I couldn't resist going out to my car to get him a China Plushky. He felt it and, for the first time, started to grasp what China looked like: "So, if the hat is here, that means this part is at the top? This is the face, right? And this is the front here?"

Brenton gave me other things to think about. "You should add the names in braille in the back and talk to the Texas School for the Blind and Visually Impaired [TSBVI]," he said. I found it quite touching to see how after I had spent years thinking about this simple concept twenty-four hours a day, a person could come into my life and open up a completely new door of possibilities. I did end up going to the TSBVI and presenting our toys. There were some magical moments when kids had new insights thanks to the Plushky they were holding, and we were able to capture those moments on camera.

The Joy of Giving

I have already given to charity more than 90 percent of those twelve thousand toys we manufactured, and I will donate most of the rest soon. The cause that has become dearest to me is the Texas School for the Blind and Visually Impaired.

The Four Seasons

One of the greatest benefits of being an entrepreneur has been all the different types of people I've met. Even though I was often seeking money, customers, or advice, I made a lot of friends from those acquaintances.

An angel investor who lived in the Four Seasons Residences in Austin was one of those who sticks in my memory. He invited me to lunch a few times, asking to hear my pitch. None of his millions moved in my direction, but he was generous with his time and insights. Further, I simply enjoyed being around someone who had such passion for life's everyday things, whether it was Internet speeds or all the construction rising around Austin.

The Forever Blessings of Friends and Family

There were many gifts to appreciate almost every day—if I was open to seeing and accepting them. Not the least of these was my parents, whose support seemingly knew no bounds. They cared for me emotionally and financially, paying for my return flights to Spain, picking me up at airports, and offering positive reinforcement over the phone.

On one visit home, I was walking around Zaragoza when I saw a toy store. I went into it and ended up talking the managers into featuring our toys in their displays. I gave them to the store for free and discovered later that my parents would drive across town to make purchases. Financially, this didn't make much sense, of course, but it was their way of providing support and creating demand, regardless of how small. My mother is still the only person on earth who I believe still pays for the toys. I have cases of inventory at home, and every time she chooses one for a gift, she leaves twenty euros in my drawer in the room where I grew up.

Another blessing was that I retained my positive attitude. I always had a *yes*. There was no job too big or too small for me. I remember having a bit of a conflict when I was putting together our Diversity Curriculum. The initial idea came from Hector and his wife, Maite, who were both teachers in Spain, but I was the one leading the project and always trying to add more value. I had a voice in my head telling me I wasn't qualified to do this, and that, as the CEO, I should be working on a big partnership and raising money. But I didn't listen to that pesky voice. Yes, it was not ideal for me to be so in the woods about creating educational materials, but it was my startup, and under the circumstances, I was the one who was going to finish the task. Entrepreneurs shouldn't only take on all the tasks they can and accept responsibility for failure or success; they should also spend some time congratulating themselves, even if it's

Entrepreneurs shouldn't only take on all the tasks they can and accept responsibility for failure or success; they should also spend some time congratulating themselves, even if it's just for the effort, for their determination in starting something new, and for their discipline continuing to do something uncomfortable and unpredictable.

just for the effort, for their determination in starting something new, and for their discipline continuing to do something uncomfortable and unpredictable.

As a founder, your company exists only because you exist. You created something and put it out into the world. Had it not been for you, the enterprise would not exist. Not many can point their finger to something visible and valuable and say, "That exists because I created it."

Such an accomplishment, even if it never makes any money, takes courage, which is often in short supply in our world. It also takes personal exposure. If your creativity and love went into the project, if your intentions were good and honorable, and if you gave it your best, failure is nothing to be ashamed of. Do not reproach yourself for not becoming Apple or Amazon or Microsoft. Instead, give yourself some appreciation for your risk and effort.

Trying our best with self-honesty is often the only thing that sustains us.

If your creativity and love went into the project, if your intentions were good and honorable, and if you gave it your best, failure is nothing to be ashamed of.

chapter 26

Is There Value in the Effort
(Even When There's None in the Results)?

....

AFTER PLUSHKIES failed, I sought solace in a number of places. Mostly, I looked for understanding and context, which I think is a normal response. I came across a quote from Eckhart Tolle that seemed amazingly appropriate for what I had just experienced: "When the ego weeps for what it has lost, the spirit rejoices for what it has found."[28]

I think that meant I was liberated from notions like the fact that getting my company to thrive was one hundred times more difficult than I had imagined. Not much went as planned, but that doesn't mean that in a broader sense there wasn't a lot that did have great value. In fact, while my company failed, my outcome was considerably brighter.

As long as I'm quoting people, let me mention John Lennon's fantastic line that, "Life is what happens to you while you are making other plans."

That was my experience.

I wanted to write a book about what I went through

Not much went as planned, but that doesn't mean that in a broader sense there wasn't a lot that did have great value. In fact, while my company failed, my outcome was considerably brighter.

because I thought that by sharing my own struggles, I might become a source of inspiration and encouragement to entrepreneurs — especially if they ever felt stuck or stupid. Maybe my thoughts and experiences could reduce their pressures and normalize their challenges. I don't know for sure, but I thought it just might be worth the effort. I did know that I didn't intend for this narrative to be about hope. My central thought was that I could tell startup entrepreneurs about the dark places in which they might end up if plans went sideways. And I thought I could be helpful if I shared how reality brought me back down to earth.

My goal was that others might learn from my hurt and be more prepared, or at least aware.

I wanted to share my experiences in dealing with emotional challenges, both as they happened at the time and with the perspective that came later through personal growth. I began to deal with the emotional fallout after I shuttered Plushkies, and I still have a long journey ahead of me. Also,

Is There Value in the Effort?

I think that trying to make my writing about hope would be a bit disingenuous. While I am hopeful, I imagine it would be difficult for readers to hear my story and be inspired and hopeful for themselves and their own pursuits.

Quite frankly, there's no way I could have made my story...inspirational.

My goal instead was to create an artifact of companionship. I wanted to help neophyte business types understand the struggles they will likely face and what they could experience as entrepreneurs. I want them to know that, more than likely, there will be moments of suffering—even if they succeed. I want to teach them to think of their projects as endeavors more than as companies or businesses. An endeavor is broader, and it suggests uncertainty as to the outcome, which we often don't think about when we start building a business. We are filled with optimism about our ideas and potential success, which is important, but so is a spoonful of reality.

Ultimately, I think the question budding entrepreneurs must answer is, *Will the effort still be worthwhile even if my company does not turn out as I envisioned it would?* What if you give everything you have out in the streets and coffee shops and in the planes and offices and conferences—and you still do not get the big dollars or the accolades for saving the world? Will it still have been worth it?

My answer to that question is *yes.*

Let me tell you why.

I recognized that I did my best with the knowledge,

Ultimately, I think the question budding entrepreneurs must answer is, Will the effort still be worthwhile even if my company does not turn out as I envisioned it would?

abilities, and resources I had at my command as a first-generation entrepreneur. I use this term because if doing something for the first time is difficult, imagine how much more trying it is if you don't know anyone in your family or among your friends or colleagues who has done or even tried to do what you are undertaking. There was no great revelation in realizing I was wasting time beating up on myself for things I might have done differently with the knowledge I now possess after going through the startup grind. I'm giving myself credit for finding a path and having the courage to walk it, then sharing the experience to prepare others who are contemplating becoming entrepreneurs. Maybe what I am offering here is a kind of emotional tool kit to provide resources that can facilitate managing a business both professionally and psychologically.

We are compelled more than we realize to keep going over our failures. Yet I refuse to indulge such a practice and won't waste my energy attempting to solve what has already happened. I also avoid any mental exercises that might detract from my current reality. I concentrate on appreciating my experience and having gratitude for finding the strength to listen to my heart (when I finally did), because it has taken me to who I am and where I am.

I think my approach had much to do with how my fortunes changed. In March 2014, as I was running out of cash for both the company and my living expenses, I ran into David Johnston at the doors of the Austin Tech Ranch. I had met him a few times previously at the Campfire meetups, and he had outlined for me his model for the vesting of employee shares in a company. I was still dreaming of growth for my startup, but at the time all I could offer was equity and commissions.

Our conversation led to him telling me about a recent trip he had taken to Amsterdam, which seemed, at least to me, out of character for David. My biased impression of him was that he was a local Austin tech company owner who was likely disinclined toward European travel. I was wrong, of course, and he related that he had attended a Bitcoin conference. Suddenly, I was curious and took up almost a half hour of his time there on the doorsteps of the Tech Ranch. He explained that Bitcoin solved the Byzantine Generals Problem—a game theory problem used to illustrate how hard it is to get consensus in distributed systems—by enabling people to find an agreement by communicating through the different components of a network in a construct that did not require a central clearing authority. In short, an exchange of value became possible without a middleman taking a cut.

When David said the phrase "the Internet of money," I became completely fixated on this new concept. Disruption like what he was describing was already proliferating, and cryptocurrencies appeared like a significant alteration of traditional business practices. I thought about how email had disrupted traditional snail mail, social media had harmed traditional newspapers, and online platforms were destroying TV viewership and music stores. Another development was that tech companies were beginning to nibble at the banking and finance space, and younger generations appeared more inclined to interact with technology firms than banks or traditional lending institutions. There was little doubt those financial giants would work to protect their positions, but I also saw how the world was becoming more digital and how the FinTech industry was becoming "a thing."

I thought money could become digital too, "why not exchange value with the same agility with which we exchange information." The "Internet of money" might win with the power of people. I wanted to get involved.

There was certainly asymmetric risk to Bitcoin, which meant there could also be big gains. The way I explained it to myself, it was ten times riskier than a gold investment but had the potential to return one hundred times more. My sense was that it was risky. Who wouldn't think a new form of currency, something that only appears every few hundred years, wouldn't be risky? And yet, at the same time, I didn't think it was as risky as it sounded because it made sense to me.

Is There Value in the Effort?

I had zero clue about how big the market might be, but I quickly became fascinated as I began buying Bitcoin and decided that these were the kinds of bets I needed to make, and that people smarter than me were going to discover its utility.

David had directed me to Coinbase to open my first account, but I was running out of cash for my own living costs and could barely afford to invest. I decided to deal with my money shortfall by taking out a $100,000 line of credit against my mortgage, which I used to support myself, finance my ongoing Plushky efforts, and invest, judiciously, in Bitcoin. As I did, my curiosity became insatiable, and I kept bothering David with basic questions. When I asked him what he recommended buying, he gave me the professional response that he was not a qualified investment advisor, which only prompted me to inquire as to what he was buying. It was a better question for both of us—David dodged the liability concern, and I knew that seeing where people put their money is much better advice than listening to the words that come out of their mouths.

David mentioned that he had his eye on the upcoming initial coin offering (ICO) for Ethereum, and I decided to participate months later with a small purchase. My hesitation was about my lack of confidence in myself, not the status of Ethereum. I had no idea what I was doing with regard to the process and the need for various passwords and files. I don't think I've ever dealt with a system that I knew less about than

I did with the Ethereum ICO. Happily, though, I jumped in and continued learning and investing, and I have continued to do so because I love the challenge, and, when the value grows, the returns are wonderful and the money is liberating.

I saw the opportunities as undeniable and kept thinking about what George Soros said: "It's not about whether you are right or wrong, but how much money you make when you are right and how much you lose when you are wrong."[29] Crypto was going to accelerate that experience because it is extremely volatile. Less than a year later, I had lost about 70 percent, and the following two years I realized tremendous gains. After that, I rode the market all the way to the bottom, which required me to reinvent my portfolio. If crypto went south, it could take me a year or two of office work to pay my new debt. If it went well, though, I might benefit from it for the rest of my life. That's the kind of asymmetric risk/reward ratio I live for. What if things went right this time, and I was able to live the life I envisioned?

I was confident to the point of almost being arrogant. I began to evangelize crypto to my closest friends and family and brought many of them into my deals. My fortunes began to rise, and I discovered a new purpose—or maybe I just revisited and reimagined a goal I'd foreseen when I first began working for the big Austin tech company. I planned to donate 1 percent of my salary each year and increase it to the point where I would be making charitable contributions with half of it by the time I reached eighty, which sounded like a good idea until I was laid off and became an entrepreneur. Suddenly, I had no income and with a company that was operating in the red, I had to completely abandon my philanthropic dreams.

Good fortune, it turns out, is constantly changing form.

A spot of success has allowed me to contemplate a new way of helping. I keep a list of the projects and dreams of my friends, family, and new acquaintances, and I have begun working on helping them make their visions come true. I look for ways to help with capital, advice, and hands-on involvement. This is more tangible and personal for me than just giving away money, and I intend to make it one of the most important projects of my life.

Good fortune, it turns out, is constantly changing form.

chapter 27

Pounding Butterflies

....

THERE IS SUCH a thing as destination addiction, and I think Americans—and the Western world in general—are quite prone to its complications. Robert Holden, PhD, a success-training coach and author, describes it as "a preoccupation with the idea that happiness is in the next place, the next job, and with the next partner. Until you give up the idea that happiness is somewhere else, it will never be where you are."[30]

We all suffer a bit from that psychology. We need to work on what we love and want to see succeed, but not to the point that it makes us miserable. There is no obligation for an entrepreneur to have a successful startup. Ambition is fine, but not when it consumes you or when your employer overrides your well-being. The less you make your happiness conditional on your startup success, the lighter you will step through your days.

I'm not saying you shouldn't take your job seriously, but I am saying be mindful of walking around with a face loaded with burden. Don't let yourself become a ghost of

> *The less you make your happiness conditional on your startup success, the lighter you will step through your days.*

the person you used to be.

A few years after I started to invest in cryptocurrencies, I had a motorbike accident. There were no significant consequences, but it was certainly scary to be lying in the middle of a street with cars passing by so close to me. I realized at least part of the cause was that there was too much banging around in my head, and I decided to quit the full-time job I had in tech. Through a cascading series of events and connections, I was in Uruguay a few months later on a six-month meditation retreat. I did not realize how much I needed such time, emotionally and physically, until I arrived at the secluded location.

Later, I wrote the first draft of this book in quarantine in the city of Cali, Colombia. During that time, I attended a three-week online retreat with spiritual teacher Jeff Foster. Much of what he taught was very relevant for this book, even though he did not mention entrepreneurship. When I scanned my notes from his class, I discovered a passage from one of his sessions that resonated with my story:

Courage is taking the step knowing it's going to be uncomfortable, and stupidity is the unwillingness to recognize that. But what changes everything is your willingness to experience that moment, the discomfort, pounding heart, the butterflies in the belly, and when you are willing to experience that, nothing can stop you. If you are willing to fully experience fear or doubt, then they cannot stop you.

I didn't have this kind of clarity or depth during my days as an entrepreneur. And if you had asked me at the time, I'd likely have said that I had already experienced enough fear and doubt, and I was done with those emotions. But that was not why I stopped being an entrepreneur. I quit because I no longer felt that's what life was asking from me. I realized it was time to do something else, regardless of the outcome I faced with Plushkies. It was time for me to have more trust in myself than in my product.

Many of us stay way too long in relationships even after we've concluded they are not working. You can also stay married to your startup far too long, convinced there will never again be such an opportunity, but this assessment limits your life before you even take the next step.

I didn't know then what I wanted to do next, and it took several more years until my Bitcoin investments accrued real value. I knew, however, that I was capable of doing almost whatever I pleased, and I wanted to work on a company or project that was functional and included a team of people who shared a similar passion. Trust was also essential—trust in myself

You can also stay married to your startup far too long, convinced there will never again be such an opportunity, but this assessment limits your life before you even take the next step.

and in others. I intended to take a step without having a specific destination. I was back to being willing to fall backward and blindfolded into the arms of life.

Following your passion isn't always the easiest or smartest route to travel. I pushed and pushed on my startup because I knew it was important to commit, and I gave it six years. Effort is important, but it is equally good and necessary to check that you are in the right lane and then recommit as often as is needed. This kind of self-reassurance will help when difficulties arise. Losing your purpose can happen faster than you are able to perceive, and you can end up with your wheels spinning, unclear of what you are trying to accomplish or why. As the ancient Chinese sage Wu Hsin taught, "One can never get enough of what does not satisfy."[31]

chapter 28

Popping the Bubble
of Idealism

....

"WE DON'T REALLY see the quitters. The heroes are the ones that persevere beyond the point of physical or emotional or mental well-being. From a narrative standpoint, we'd prefer somebody to push past the point of sensibility and perseverance and actually perish to somebody who rightly quits early.

"Rob Hall, who was an amazing alpinist and expedition leader, was one of those people who broke the turnaround time—the latest set time to reach a checkpoint or turn-around—climbing Mount Everest and perished. And what's really interesting is that there were some people who followed the turnaround time, made these great decisions, and nobody remembers their names. And that's part of the problem. How do you get people like that to be the hero of your narrative?"[32] This is an edited extract of the fascinating conversation ex-professional poker player Annie Duke had with Maya Shankar in Maya's podcast *A Slight Change of Plans*.

Desire and Foundations

We get so attached to our desires that it becomes very hard to let them go. We make desires such a part of our foundation that we unconsciously believe that to question them becomes an invitation to deeply question ourselves, and there is a part of us that wants nothing less than to be questioned at that level.

The hero enjoys being in control fighting to confirm his activity. He doesn't want to question his identity because that would mean lowering the head, letting go of the ego, and accepting there are things he doesn't know.

> *There is a time to pop the bubble of idealism and listen to reality with clarity, understanding what is and what is not possible. That is humility.*

There is a time to pop the bubble of idealism and listen to reality with clarity, understanding what is and what is not possible. That is humility.

Humility can help us organize our own human limits and resources. There is a pole in us entrepreneurs that deeply rejects the idea of having limits. That Peter Pan place in us that tells us anything is possible. Limits to our desires (such us desire for my startup success) may come up. What will then be the kindest act for my energy and self-regulation?

When hitting this wall, the work is in recognizing that even though there are many possibilities for us, not everything is possible. Or, at the very least, it's not wise to pursue some of them. I can try to do anything—yes, I could still try to be a professional soccer player, but at what cost?

Order and Software

There are pursuits that have to do with will and others that have to do with rules that belong to an order we don't intellectually understand.

Our human side that fights is not allowing itself to be touched by reality. The clash with our idea of how things should be invites us to humility. Perhaps I'm not seeing the whole picture. Are we open to doubting our beliefs that reality is not confirming?

Assuming there is a human experience I'm not going to explore enables me to discover the human experience I now need to develop.

Assuming there is a human experience I'm not going to explore enables me to discover the human experience I now need to develop. To recognize when life is telling you, "Up to here," because at the same time it's pointing somewhere else and telling you, "Here, this way."

If your mind is too stubborn, you stop listening to what life is trying to tell you. So we need to develop the sensibility to differentiate between a challenge to overcome and life itself, saying, "Not this way, but I invite you to explore this other thing."

If your mind is too stubborn, you stop listening to what life is trying to tell you. So we need to develop the sensibility to differentiate between a challenge to overcome and life itself, saying, "Not this way, but I invite you to explore this other thing."

What life is stripping is a program that no longer works, but the old parts of us that have been "using" this program for years will suffer. This programming that was useful up this point needs to fall out so a new one that's more suitable for what's next can appear.

As we learn to register life, the operating system that wants to be installed is of higher sensitivity and less existential myopia.

The Wise and the Hero

The challenges we experience can turn into a hero's journey, fighting with reality, or they can be clues to feel life and reality as great pointers. To make this movement one puts their desire out in the world but with the humility of not knowing where life will take you.

Wise people have traditionally been contemplators of life, and showcased with an understanding of life that is not only based in moving in it through sheer will and cleverness to achieve their aims, but a capacity to meaningfully listen—and even communicate—to it.

The grand art between contemplation and intervention opens us to a deeper level of involvement. If life was trying to send me a message through all these experiences, what would it be? There are times to commit, to recommit, and even to self-actualize again and have the courage to ask yourself, *What makes the most sense now?* And it may well be that the answer is to take a break from what you have been doing for many years and be open to something, even though you don't yet know what it is.

In a surprising development after I put my startup to sleep, I had the chance to talk about it with Sir Richard Branson, the British founder of the Virgin Group and a commercial astronaut. I was able to speak with him on Necker Island, his island in the Caribbean, at a gathering of entre-preneurs, which gave us privacy and the comfort of speaking openly. When I mentioned the idea of this book, we began a back-and-forth.

"I think it takes a lot of courage to start a company," I said. "I also think it takes a lot of courage when you've given everything to the company and if it hasn't succeeded, to move on. I wanted to ask you at what point would you advise a person to walk away, even though they are still in love with the idea but it is not working out?"

"I've met a lot of very interesting people whose ideas have not worked out," Branson said. "The people who try and don't succeed often have much more interesting stories to tell than the people who try and actually do succeed. And I actually thought about putting together stories about people who tried and failed into a book. So, I really look forward to reading your book. It's much more exciting to read a book about someone who has gone into all the battles and the challenges.

"So, when to call it a day? I've had many occasions when I stuck with a company too long, and it cost us a lot of money when I should have called it a day earlier on, so I can sympathize with you. You really need to call it a day when you are about to get kicked out of your house. If you are going to come back to it and do it again, you are likely going to have to take a twist to the idea; it sounds like a lovely idea. Maybe you need to pitch it to a games company, but I definitely want to read your book."

"Thank you very much," I said. "I've already moved on. And what words of wisdom would you have for an entrepreneur who gave his everything and it didn't work out?"

"Oh, my words are simply to do exactly as you have done, and that is pick yourself up, brush yourself off, and try again. Is that what you do?"

"Yeah, I did."

"And if the next one fails," Branson said, "try again and keep going until you are successful. That's what I had to do in the early part of my life. You are learning. If you are going to write a book, you are going to have a lot of the mistakes you made in the story, and maybe you won't make the same mistakes next time around, and maybe your next book will be shorter."

Maybe, I thought, *my next book will be about success.*

Afterword

....

I WANT TO finish this book with a parable, because I think the story nicely illuminates how we can often overlook the obvious when we are distracted by problems. Our noses can be so close to the grindstone that we lose sight of what we were initially trying to create or accomplish.

Once there was a king who received a gift of two magnificent falcons from Arabia. They were peregrine falcons, the most beautiful birds he had ever seen. He gave the precious birds to his head falconer to be trained.

Months passed and one day the head falconer informed the king that though one of the falcons was flying majestically, soaring high in the sky, the other bird had not moved from its branch since the day it had arrived.

The king summoned healers and sorcerers from all the land to tend to the falcon, but no one could make the bird fly. He presented the task to a member of his court, but the next day, the king saw through the palace window that the bird had still not moved from its perch. Having tried everything else, the king thought to himself, *Maybe I need someone more familiar with the countryside to understand the nature of this problem.* So he cried out to his court, "Go and get a farmer."

In the morning, the king was thrilled to see the falcon soaring high above the palace gardens. He said to his court, "Bring me the doer of this miracle."

The court quickly located the farmer, who came and stood before the king. The king asked him, "How did you make the falcon fly?"

With head bowed, the farmer said to the king, "It was very easy, your highness. I simply cut the branch of the tree where the bird was sitting, and it started to fly."[33]

There is a lesson in that brief narrative—and not just for startup businesspeople. I learned from experience that entrepreneurship is hard, and there are many reasons for those challenges. These include figuring out product and market fit, finding the right team, discovering compatible investors, and creating effective marketing and messaging. All these challenges point to the enterprise and not to the entrepreneur. I think we know a great deal about startups as enterprises, but what happens to the entrepreneur has been less studied.

How do you feel after using every drop of gas you have in the tank if your product does not work as expected? Not good, I can tell you that much.

What if it's impossible to reach your buyers? What if your cofounder and you stop seeing eye to eye? What if your well-laid plans don't last more than a couple of days? What if you end up feeling like a shadow of your old self?

What was in front of

We can often overlook the obvious when we are distracted by problems. Our noses can be so close to the grindstone that we lose sight of what we were initially trying to create or accomplish.

me was not satisfying, even though I had always wanted to be an entrepreneur. I wanted it before I even knew the word for it. I prepared by cultivating my ambitions and reading many books about entrepreneurship and tech. I also took many entrepreneurship classes while I was getting my MBA.

Each of our experiences in business is unique, but I am hopeful that potential entrepreneurs will see themselves in what I went through and will learn without my level of suffering. There is zero doubt that some of this will apply to you, but I don't want to deter anyone from the adventure that could lead to taking control of their own future. I hope that persistence is my message, and that no one gives up their dream of the future—but hopefully they are more realistic about what is required and all the attendant risks than I was.

There will be moments when things seem to fit, when everything flows and disparate parts are pulled together by cosmic magic. Then . . .there are those times when all you see before you every morning is a struggle, that life is unfair and the world is against you.

When we have emotional responses to situations, we fail to pay attention to how our body is operating and what it's going through because we are so focused on business. We feel we have no time to contemplate our emotions. But if we don't take care of our emotional selves, those raw emotions will fester and grow, spreading their dark tendrils throughout every part of our lives. Our businesses, our relationships, and our physical and emotional health can all start falling apart.

Our body talks to us. If we don't listen to its subtle messages, it will try harder until we do—and we might be the last to notice how urgent the situation has become.

I think we get into situations where we act out our fears while running our companies, and that happens almost unconsciously with bad decisions caused by a lack of clarity and depression. We begin to doubt ourselves and our capabilities and think that life is unfair or that we've made a poor choice for our startup. These currents of thought can act as self-fulfilling prophecies and create an emotional state that overwhelms and paralyzes us.

Entrepreneurs tend to get into these painful situations because they associate their self-worth with the success of their companies. Allowing yourself to be defined by an entity so small as your startup is a major mistake, regardless of how big your dreams might be. Don't let the success or failure of your venture define your character; those two dynamics are not interdependent. I realize that is much easier to write than do, but at least try to maintain an awareness of that kind of thinking. I allowed my happiness and peace of mind to depend on the traction of Plushkies, and that was one of my greatest failures.

There will be moments when things seem to fit, when everything flows and disparate parts are pulled together by cosmic magic. Then...there are those times when all you see before you every morning is a struggle, that life is unfair and the world is against you.

Afterword

Don't let the success or failure of your venture define your character; those two dynamics are not interdependent.

Don't be your start-up's bitch. Don't get dizzy bouncing around the ring. On the contrary, use your company—along with all the significance you gave it, its disappointments, and all its challenges—to enhance your personal growth. To become *more*—more open, more skillful, more sensitive, and more productive. Be the master of yourself as much as the leader of your business. Get better at your craft and try to feel personal growth as an entrepreneur, no matter the destiny of your company. Keep improving. Study people such as Jobs and Musk. Apply what serves your goals while leaving what doesn't. Don't try to become someone you are not. Trust your intentions and your intuition on what is best for you and your business. Take counsel when needed but make the hard decisions. Remember the maxim, "Easy decisions, hard life. Hard decisions, easy life."

Be careful of the risk of getting too enamored of your company. Remember that you are so much more than just your startup. In my view, we have but two real purposes in our lives, and the most important is to discover who we really are. Keep sight of that as you push your business vision, because the other purpose I think we possess is to contribute to the wider world with our talents and skills, which allows us to live our truest and fullest lives.

As entrepreneurs, we put all of our efforts and heart into building, serving, and making a mark in the world. Whether that happens or not, use your entrepreneurial experience for your growth, for your deeper understanding of who you are. I'm not talking about an intellectual understanding, but an *experiential* one. Whether you can give your gift to the world in the form you want or not, there is something much more important than giving your gift to others, and that is being true to yourself, to your core being.

Use your company— along with all the significance you gave it, its disappointments, and all its challenges—to enhance your personal growth. To become more— *more open, more skillful, more sensitive, and more productive.*

We don't need more technology to bail out planet Earth. We don't require a once-in-a-generation software genius or a new mega-engineering ecoventure to save us all, but we do need to treat one another well and take care of ourselves. Take personal responsibility, and don't expect someone else to do for you what you haven't been able to do for yourself.

Be careful of the risk of getting too enamored of your company. Remember that you are so much more than just your startup.

Use your entrepreneurial experience for your growth, for your deeper understanding of who you are.

What good does powerful innovation do in the hands of someone who is never satisfied? How is an entrepreneur who doesn't understand themself going to treat the planet? What would a chaotic mind most likely manifest in the world?

It's easy to be harshly critical of yourself when you don't experience the degree of success you anticipated. But can you be kind to yourself in the midst of what you view as failure?

I do believe in sacrifice, though the word is not very appealing to me. I can see value in making sacrifices to facilitate our growth and push the limits to become more than we thought possible. But don't make the mistake of using your sacrifices to justify your misery. You make sacrifices to achieve goals, not to stay trapped in a cage of unhappiness. Life must be about more than sacrifice and burnout.

Nothing you have read here should deter you from starting out with your new enterprise. Put yourself on the line and go build your company. Don't give up too quickly. Try. And try again. Be focused. Try again. And

Don't give up too quickly. Try. And try again. Be focused. Try again. And again, and again. Make sure you leave everything on the dance floor.

again, and again. Make sure you leave everything on the dance floor. Don't become obsessed with fear of failure. Very few people have the product I spent six years trying to sell, and the world seems to be doing just fine without it. (I even seem to be doing fine as well :)

The markets may not receive your startup as you expected, but you and your contributions as a person will always have value.

And listen to life, because life knows that you are much more than your startup, much more even than your founder dreams.

The world doesn't need your startup; the world needs you.

Stop saving the world and start saving yourself.

Few things in life will get you closer to your full expression, depth, and maturity than being a self-aware entrepreneur.

Not just because you want to "make the world a better place," but because you want to come closer to who you truly are. And few things in life will get you closer to your full expression, depth, and maturity than being a self-aware entrepreneur.

You may have a "successful" company, but what do you have if you don't have yourself?

Honor your precious and sacred life. Appreciate and take care of yourself.

Pause for a second in the middle of the turmoil of entrepreneurship and life and notice what you are deeply and honestly going through right in this moment. And stay with yourself there.

That's the (kind of) company you need. And we all need it too.

Notes

1. Josh Howarth, "Startup Failure Rate Statistics (2024)," *Exploding Topics* (blog), November 3, 2023, https://explodingtopics.com/blog/startup-failure-stats.

2. Tim Ferriss, "How to Create Your Own Real-World MBA," *Tim Ferris* (blog), June 28, 2010, https://tim.blog/2010/06/28/mba/.

3. Guy Kawasaki, "Make Meaning in Your Company," eCorner, October 20, 2004, https://ecorner.stanford.edu/videos/make-meaning-in-your-company/.

4. Josh Howarth, "Startup Failure Rate Statistics (2024)," *Exploding Topics* (blog), November 3, 2023, https://explodingtopics.com/blog/startup-failure-stats.

5. "Mindset of a millionaire," @mindset.of.a.millionaire, Instagram, December 4, 2023, https://www.instagram.com/reel/C0cIE_pNUKf/?igsh=Y21tOHVncDI0YXhq.

6. "Steve Jobs' dent in the universe—the shocking truth revealed!" Solve/Next, https://solvenext.com/blog/steve-jobs-dent-in-the-universethe-shocking-truth-revealed.

7. Entrepreneur, author, TED speaker, and owner of rejectiontherapy.com/.

8. https://www.youtube.com/watch?v=wH4cv1e1MvU

9. Rob Henderson, "America Exports Cancel Culture to the World," Quillette, July 2, 2020, https://quillette.com/2020/07/02/america-exports-cancel-culture-to-the-world/.

10. Jeff Foster, *Deep Rest Course*, Session 5, Minute 5:15.

11. Jeff Foster, *Deep Rest Course*, Session 5, Minute 25.

12. "Reject Most Advice," Naval, May 20, 2019, https://nav.al/reject-advice.

13. Dr. Joe Dispenza, "Back to Basics," Dr. Joe Dispenza, August 1, 2020,

Notes

https://drjoedispenza.com/dr-joes-blog/back-to-basics.

14. *MindsetVibrations*, YouTube, May 31, 2023, https://www.youtube.com/shorts/nTVa1lzVZzE.

15. "In Order to Change Your Life, You Need to Learn This First!" Be Inspired, June 20, 2018, https://www.youtube.com/watch?v=wvWUpHv4AXs.

16. Angela Lee Duckworth, "Grit: the Power of Passion and Perseverance," TED, May 9, 2013, https://www.youtube.com/watch?v=H14bBuluwB8.

17. "Be Good," Paul Graham, April 2008, https://paulgraham.com/good.html.

18. "From Silicon Valley to Barcelona: building scaleups with global ambition," Tech Barcelona, https://www.youtube.com/watch?v=1RdDJaHaI8w.

19. Tim Ferriss, "How to Say No When It Matters Most (or Why I'm Taking a Long 'Startup Vacation')," *Tim Ferriss* (blog), October 29, 2015, https://tim.blog/2015/10/29/startup-vacation-2/.

20. Susan Peppercorn, PCC, "How to Rebound from Failure Like a Scientist," LinkedIn, October 8, 2017, https://www.linkedin.com/pulse/how-rebound-from-failure-like-scientist-susan-peppercorn/.

21. Geoffrey A. Moore, *Crossing the Chasm*, Wikipedia, https://en.wikipedia.org/wiki/Crossing_the_Chasm.

22. Charlotte Schallenberg, "Extending the 'Pepsi Paradox' to Diet Cola," University of South Carolina, https://sc.edu/about/offices_and_divisions/research/news_and_pubs/caravel/archive/2015/2015-caravel-pepsi-paradox.php.

23. Matthew Yglesias, "Sweet Sorrow: Coke won the cola wars because great taste takes more than a single sip," *Slate*, August 9, 2013, https://slate.com/business/2013/08/pepsi-paradox-why-people-prefer-coke-even-though-pepsi-wins-in-taste-tests.html.

24. Ian Winwood, "'Sometimes I feel that it's the most honest record I ever made...' The story of Green Day's Insomniac," Kerrang! October 8, 2021, https://www.kerrang.com/green-day-the-inside-story-of-insomniac.

25. Law of Attraction Academy, Quantum Observers Instagram Page, November 16, 2023, https://www.instagram.com/reel/CzuOYh0s-s3/.

26. https://www.digitaldetox.com/experiences/camp-grounded/.

27. Huberman Diaries, Instagram, November 29, 2023, https://www.instagram.com/reel/C0ODGlloDie/

Notes

28. "There's a Saying," Sloww, Twitter Post, March 27, 2020, https://twitter
    .com/SlowwCo/status/1243630030908878848.

29. "6 Best George Soros Quotes on Successful Investing" Fincash, updated
    February 18, 2024, https://www.fincash.com/l/investment
    /george-soros-quotes-on-successful-investing.

30. Robert Holden Daily Quotes, RobertHolden.com, September
    19, 2023, https://www.robertholden.com/daily-quotes/
    beware-of-destination-addiction/.

31. "Wu Hsin—The Absolute Understanding," Corvo Seco YouTube Channel,
    April 18, 2021, https://www.youtube.com/watch?v=OF0D8FpqOmQ.

32. Dr. Maya Shankar, "The Science of Quitting," A Slight Change of
    Plans (podcast), accessed February 24, 2024, https://www.pushkin
    .fm/podcasts/a-slight-change-of-plans/the-science-of-quitting.

33. "The Two Falcons," Daily Ten Minutes, https://www.dailytenminutes.
    com/2015/06/story-two-falcons.html.

Acknowledgments

I'D LIKE TO acknowledge all company founders and all those who supported us when we were not treading on the most conventional or socially acceptable paths.

To those who believed in *us* even when they didn't believe in what we *did*—thanks for accepting that giving us freedom and encouragement to express ourselves in the playground of creation was more relevant than meeting any expectations you had for us.

Writing this book has felt like a startup. It doesn't matter what you produce—toys, books, shoes—there are always two common elements in the process: the making and the marketing. I have so many people to thank for both that I'd need to write another book just for that. And that's including myself, since at times I felt as if I had to read my own book to remind me of some of the lessons in it.

James Moore, what a wise man and sincere friend you are. I'll always remember your first words after reading my manuscript: "This story needs to be told, but this book needs to be rewritten." *Yikes!* Thanks for not succumbing to the

Acknowledgments

daunting task of those first edits and being available for me every step of the way.

Thanks to the very early supporters of this book. Those people will likely be surprised to be mentioned here because we seemingly had a "passing interaction," but they provided critical contributions to give me visibility, structure, and confidence in a process that, if followed, would bring my book to completion.

Thanks to my friend Charlie Hoehn for pointing me to a book-writing webinar that author Tucker Max was about to give at the beginning of the pandemic at a time when I was as committed to this book as I was lost in how to best move forward. And thanks again, Charlie, for your most recent suggestions that allowed me to wrap up the book with liberating confidence.

The webinar I mentioned was packed with equal parts information and motivation. I still remember Tucker sending us all a message along the lines of "in a few years you will look back at the pandemic, and what you do with this time can really matter." His encouragement allowed the participants to use that time to write our books.

Emily Gindlesparger and Hal Clifford, thanks for the community of authors you sustained in 2020 with your weekly calls full of patience and wisdom. And thanks for your sensible and sensitive feedback when my manuscript was still raw.

Thanks to Forefront Books for bringing this book to the finish line. Thanks to Jonathan Merkh for coming to the rescue

Acknowledgments

and taking me under your wing at a challenging time during which the book needed a new direction and I needed someone I could trust. Thanks to Jennifer Gingerich for your professionalism holding the reins of the project, providing direction, understanding, and common sense, and to Allen Harris for adding value and insights with your edits—beyond what I knew was possible. I'm grateful to all the others at Forefront Books who contributed their creativity and hard work, from designer to editors and everyone else.

Thanks to all my family and friends who gave me feedback on the manuscript, cover concepts, and subtitles. I ask for a special request for sympathy if your preferences were not reflected in the cover. :)

Thanks to all those old friends—or characters—who are featured in the book, and thanks to the new friends who are founders, investors, or work with media who are excited about how this book can make a difference to entrepreneurs, if only by providing a touch of clarity, comfort, and recognition.

A special callout goes to Cesar Camacho for your support, vision, and enthusiasm, and to Aurora for our magical and therapeutic conversations, which I have woven into the last chapter of this book. I believe they can be as illuminating to other founders who are ready to question some of their ideas as they were to me.

Thanks to Fuqua School of Business at Duke for the friends I made, for the opportunity of becoming part of my first startup, and for opening a world of possibility that

Acknowledgments

resonated with my heart and ambition. Howie Rhee, I admire your capacity to keep the names of hundreds of Duke students and alumni in your head and for adding so much value to us all through your targeted connections.

And finally, thanks to all those who touched my career or personal life even before this book, or even before Juan—without whom this story would have never taken place—and I started bouncing ideas off of each other for our company. I extend my gratitude from our hometown of Zaragoza, Spain, to London, UK, from Austin, Texas, to Indonesia, from Uruguay and Colombia to Durham, North Carolina. These are all special places in my heart that forged the story before there was one on paper.

Thanks to everybody's love for my human experience in its perfection.